Discovery of the Americas, 1492–1800

Revised Edition

DISCOVERY & EXPLORATION

Discovery of the Americas, 1492–1800
Revised Edition

TOM SMITH

JOHN S. BOWMAN and MAURICE ISSERMAN
General Editors

CHELSEA HOUSE
PUBLISHERS
An imprint of Infobase Publishing

Discovery of the Americas, 1492–1800, Revised Edition

Copyright ©2010 by Infobase Publishing

Chelsea House
An imprint of Infobase Publishing
132 West 31st Street
New York NY 10001

Library of Congress Cataloging-in-Publication Data
Smith, Tom, 1953-
 Discovery of the Americas, 1492-1800 / by Tom Smith. -- Rev. ed.
  p. cm.
 Includes bibliographical references and index.
 ISBN 978-1-60413-195-6 (hardcover)
 1. America--Discovery and exploration--Juvenile literature. 2. Explorers--America--History--Juvenile literature. 3. Explorers--America--Biography--Juvenile literature. I. Title.

 E101.S65 2005
 973.1--dc22
                        2009022330

Chelsea House books are available at special discounts when purchased in bulk quantities for businesses, associations, institutions, or sales promotions. Please call our Special Sales Department in New York at (212) 967-8800 or (800) 322-8755.

You can find Chelsea House on the World Wide Web at
http://www.chelseahouse.com

Text design by Erika K. Arroyo
Cover design by Keith Trego
Composition by EJB Publishing Services
Cover printed by Bang Printing, Brainerd, MN
Book printed and bound by Bang Printing, Brainerd, MN
Date printed: November 2009
Printed in the United States of America

10 9 8 7 6 5 4 3 2 1

This book is printed on acid-free paper.

All links and Web addresses were checked and verified to be correct at the time of publication. Because of the dynamic nature of the Web, some addresses and links may have changed since publication and may no longer be valid.

Contents

1

Columbus Returns to Spain

THE LETTER IN CHRISTOPHER COLUMBUS'S HANDS ERASED YEARS of rejection and ridicule by everyone who had doubted him. It was from King Ferdinand II of Aragon and Queen Isabella I of Castile, the sovereign rulers of Spain. The letter was addressed to "Don Cristóbal Colón, their Admiral of the Ocean Sea, Viceroy and Governor of the Islands that he hath discovered in the Indies." Columbus—called Colón in Spain—had spent most of the past year at sea looking for a westward passage from Europe to Asia. Having sailed among islands he named "the Indies," he sent messages to the Spanish rulers as soon as he returned. He announced that his mission had been a success. Columbus knew the rewards he had insisted upon receiving if his voyage was successful were now his.

The letter was dated March 30, 1493. When Columbus opened it, he read that King Ferdinand and Queen Isabella wanted to see him as quickly as possible:

> We have seen your letters and we have taken much pleasure in learning whereof you write, and that God gave so good a result to your labors, and well guided you in what you commenced, whereof He will be well served and we also, and our realms receive so much advantage. It will please God that, beyond that wherein you serve Him, you should receive from us many favors ... we desire that you come here forthwith, therefore for our service make the best haste you can in your coming, so that you may be timely provided

with everything you need; and because as you see the summer has begun, and you must not delay in going back there, see if something cannot be prepared in Seville or in other districts for your returning to the land which you have discovered.

There had never been any doubt in Columbus's mind that he would reach Asia by sailing west. He would now present his proof at the royal court at Barcelona, showing everyone that he was neither a dreamer nor crazy.

THE ROAD TO BARCELONA

This moment was years in the making. After a lifetime of sailing the seas off Europe and West Africa, studying navigational theories, and poring over maps, he was convinced that reaching "the Indies" was possible. However, Columbus's dream had been stalled. The leaders of Portugal, France, and England rejected his proposals. The Spanish rulers rejected him twice over a period of eight years before giving him the meager resources with which he accomplished his feat.

At sea he had endured weeks of worry. His restless crew could mutiny at any moment and demand a return to Spain. His flagship, the *Santa Maria*, had been wrecked and abandoned. Violent storms nearly sent his remaining two ships to the bottom of the Atlantic Ocean on the voyage home. His men had been arrested by Portuguese authorities in the Azores. Then, stopping in Portugal on the way home, Columbus had escaped Portuguese courtiers who wanted their king to have the mariner killed. They wanted to prevent news of his success from becoming known. Against tremendous odds, Columbus was now safely in Spain. He could not wait to describe his discoveries to the king and queen.

A FACE IN THE CROWD

When Columbus rode through the streets of Barcelona on April 20, 1493, one of the onlookers was 18-year-old Bartolomé de Las Casas. The young man's father later sailed with Columbus when the admiral returned to "the Indies." Bartolomé himself would later immigrate to Cuba to work as a planter. He then became the first priest ordained in the Western Hemisphere, a historian, and a defender of the rights of Native Americans.

Hoping to locate a western route to the Indies to find jewels and spices, Columbus presented his plans to the rulers of Portugal, Genoa, Venice, England, and Spain. All turned him down. Finally, after two years of negotiations, Spain's King Ferdinand and Queen Isabella agreed to finance half of his voyage. Above, Ferdinand and Isabella receive Columbus at court in 1493 after his first voyage to the Americas.

Las Casas watched Columbus closely over the years and would become close to his brothers and sons. By the time his book, *History of the Indies,* was completed more than 70 years later, Las Casas had personally known many famous (and infamous) explorers. Among them were Hernán Cortés, Vasco Núñez de Balboa, Juan Ponce de León, Pánfilo de Narváez, and Ferdinand Magellan. These men and other figures played great and small parts in Spain's age of discovery. Las Casas found much to both admire and criticize in Christopher Columbus.

On that day in 1493, however, young Las Casas joined the crowd watching Columbus. "The entire city came out, so that there was not room for all the people in the streets," he wrote. "All wondered to see that venerable person who was said to have discovered another world; to see the Indians, parrots, jewels, and gold things he had discovered."

Columbus reached a platform built to receive him in full public view. King Ferdinand and Queen Isabella arrived. They were surrounded by noblemen and religious officials. Columbus kneeled and kissed their hands as a sign of respect.

The admiral presented the rulers with his proof. It could only have come from exotic lands. "Don Christopher Columbus," remembered Las Casas, "carried very beautiful red-tinged green parrots, and guaycas, which were masks made of a collection of fishbones arranged like pearl-seed, and some belts of the same material, fashioned with admirable craftsmanship; also a great quantity and variety of very fine gold, and many other things never before seen or heard of in Spain."

Columbus described the wide bays and forested mountains of the Indies. He told of islands that would one day be named the Bahamas, Cuba, and Hispaniola (home to the nations of Haiti and the Dominican Republic). He presented gifts of jewelry. "He asserted," Las Casas wrote, "the infinite amount of gold shown in those lands and his confidence that it would restore the royal treasury—as if he had already collected it and deposited it under his keys. And likewise what was of greater weight and a rare treasure, he described the multitude, simplicity, mildness, nakedness, and certain customs of their peoples, and their fit disposition and capability . . . for being led to our holy faith."

Columbus had kidnapped about 20 Taino people from their home islands and brought them to Spain. He planned to teach them Spanish and use them as interpreters. Most had died during the difficult voyage. Seven survivors, now baptized, were presented to the court. Months earlier, these same Taino men had stood on faraway beaches. They marveled at the strange beards, heavy garments, and pale skin of the tall men who had appeared in their midst. Now, the short, beardless Taino were the center of attention.

DREAMS AND NIGHTMARES OF A NEW WORLD

At the same moment Columbus was telling tales of beautiful islands full of gold, a nightmare was unfolding at La Navidad. This was the outpost he had left on the northern coast of Haiti. Columbus had told 39 volunteers to build a colony there. When Columbus sailed for Spain, the colonists brutalized the Taino. They ordered them to provide the outpost with more food and gold. The colonists would later pay for this arrogance with their lives.

In Barcelona on the day of Columbus's arrival at the Spanish court, however, the people rejoiced. They thought about great things to come. The rulers finished listening to their guest's tales of the Indies. The singers of the royal chapel were signaled to chant the Christian hymn *Te Deum*. There were tears in the eyes of the monarchs, Columbus, and others present.

THE PEOPLE WHO GREETED COLUMBUS

The first people Columbus met in the Americas were Taino. They were one of a group of Caribbean tribes linked by the common use of the Arawak language. Arawak speakers lived throughout the Caribbean, from the southern tip of Florida to islands off the northern coast of South America. Numerous words from Arawak are used today, including *canoe, tobacco, hammock, iguana,* and *Haiti.* The Arawak-speaking tribes depended mainly on fishing and farming for survival. Their peaceful society made them easily exploitable by Spanish colonists, who replaced their previous major threat, the Carib.

The Carib were a seagoing tribe from the Lesser Antilles islands (which includes the Leeward Islands, Trinidad and Tobago, Barbados, and islands off the northern coast of Venezuela). A branch of the tribe also lived on the northeastern coastline of South America. The Taino people accused the Carib of being cannibals.

Columbus's men clashed with the Carib while exploring the waters surrounding St. Croix. Columbus had promised the Taino of Hispaniola that the rulers of Spain would destroy the Carib. Within 100 years, however, both the Arawak and Carib cultures had been wiped out. They were killed by European diseases, forced labor, and wars lost to Spanish colonists.

After the ceremony, Columbus was shown to his lodgings. The admiral was thinking ahead. He was ready to set sail again. He meant to follow the islands he had discovered to the court of the Grand Khan of China or to the imperial palaces of Japan. Columbus was already planning to set sail toward the western horizon.

A NEW WORLD

News of Columbus's first voyage spread across southern Europe with surprising speed. Columbus's written report to Ferdinand and Isabella, later known as his "Letter on the First Voyage," reached Barcelona so quickly that it was printed and distributed publicly even before his arrival at court. Gradually, copies of his report were seen throughout Europe. Many believed that the islands Columbus had reached lay off the eastern shores of Asia. Such scholars included Queen Isabella's chaplain, an Italian priest and geographer named Pietro Martire d'Anghiera. Better known as Peter Martyr, he was both fascinated by and skeptical of the admiral's grand claims. Martyr wrote:

> A certain Colonus [Columbus] has . . . discovered many islands which are thought to be those of which mention is made by cosmographers, beyond the eastern ocean and adjacent to India. I do not wholly deny this, although the size of the globe seems to suggest otherwise, for there are not wanting those who think the Indian coast to be a short distance from the end of Spain. . . . Enough for us that the hidden half of the globe is brought to light, and the Portuguese daily go farther and farther beyond the equator. Thus shores hitherto unknown will soon become accessible.

Peter Martyr had no way of knowing what Columbus's discovery would mean to the course of human history. His skepticism about Columbus's claims faded as he studied the western voyages. He also met explorers like Vasco Núñez de Balboa and Antón de Alaminos. Martyr learned a great deal about the civilizations of the Americas. Writing extensively after 1511, his findings spread throughout Europe. In 1530, four years after his death, his collected writings were published in Latin under the title *De Orbe Novo*—"The New World." This phrase was used by future generations to describe the Western Hemisphere. By then, Europeans accepted that the Americas were not part of Asia.

Columbus never accepted this. He once wrote in his journal that he had discovered "a very great continent which until today has been unknown." He even referred to it as "an Other World." He remained convinced that he could find a landmass linking it to China. Many years would pass before anyone on either side of the Atlantic Ocean would realize how wrong he was, yet how important his mistake would become.

2

The Four Voyages of Columbus

WHILE COLUMBUS WAS WRONG TO ASSUME THAT HE HAD discovered an uncomplicated paradise, at that moment a combination of politics, religion, and technology increased the chance that the Spanish would be the first to open a busy route between Europe and the Americas. In 1492, the nations of Europe's Mediterranean coast explored more than any other nation in the world. China, whose skilled mariners and sturdy ships had journeyed to Arabia and the coast of East Africa, had withdrawn from long-distance voyaging in the early 1400s. Arab mariners had settled into a routine of seasonal travel to trading ports in India and the South China Sea. By 1492, many Asians and Arabians were aware of Europe. They had little interest, however, in making any sea voyages beyond their immediate regions.

Geographical exploration was a serious business. The cities of northern Italy were home to the best schools of mapmaking. The Italian-born explorers of the late 1400s and 1500s included Columbus, Amerigo Vespucci, John Cabot (Giovanni Caboto), and Giovanni da Verrazano. Yet, with the exception of Verrazano, who was backed by France, all of these men sailed for Spain.

EUROPEANS TAKE TO THE SEA

The explorers' crews came mostly from Portugal or Spain. The ports in these countries offered many experienced sailors and pilots. Portuguese captains trained under Prince Henry the Navigator. He had founded an important school of navigational and geographical studies in southwestern Portugal.

In 1492, Spain's merchants were wealthy. They wanted to find a way to purchase valuable spices and silk directly from Asian suppliers. Buying direct would allow them to pay less than they paid to the Arab traders who sold goods to Europeans in Egyptian markets. Meanwhile, the Portuguese were looking for such a route by rounding Africa into the Indian Ocean. They had no interest in a dreamer like Columbus.

SAILOR FROM GENOA

Christopher Columbus was born Cristoforo Colombo in Genoa in 1451. Genoa was a powerful city-state that did not formally become part of the nation of Italy until 1861. Columbus was born into a family of woolen merchants. By the time he was a young man, he had become an experienced sailor. He had traveled throughout the Mediterranean, south to West Africa, and north as far as England, Ireland, and the waters off Iceland.

No one knows how Columbus decided it was possible to sail west to Asia. It is known that Columbus corresponded with Paulo Toscanelli. Toscanelli was a respected scholar from Florence who believed that Asia could be reached by sailing west. He had provided the king of Portugal with a world map upon which an ocean separated the coasts of Europe and Asia. The map, however, depicted nothing but open sea where the Americas lie and greatly underestimated the distance between the Canary Islands and Japan. Toscanelli thought they were only 3,000 nautical miles (3,452 miles or 5,555 km) apart. In reality, they are separated by 10,600 miles (17,059 km).

Columbus made his own calculations. He studied the work of French cardinal Pierre d'Ailly. D'Ailly believed that Spain and India were within sailing distance of each other. Columbus calculated the distance between Japan and Europe to be a mere 2,400 nautical miles (2,761 miles or 4,443 km). Although this was a great distance to mariners of the era, Columbus's belief that he would encounter islands along the way made it seem worth the risk.

All fifteenth-century geographers underestimated the circumference of Earth. Columbus's faulty calculations determined that Earth was only 25 percent of its actual size. Had his calculations been closer to the truth, it is unlikely he could have convinced anyone to fund his voyage.

This portrait is believed to be of Columbus in 1519, created by Sebastiano del Piombo 14 years after the explorer's death.

SEARCHING FOR A PATRON

Columbus waited for years before he found a sponsor for his first voyage. He first applied for backing to João II, king of Portugal, but was unsuccessful. Then he journeyed to Spain. In 1486, he met with the king and queen, Ferdinand of Aragon and Isabella of Castile. Instead of giving him backing for his voyage, Isabella referred his proposal to a group of scholars called the Talavera Commission. After several years of study, the Talavera Commission told the Spanish sovereigns, "We can find no justification for their Highnesses' supporting a project that rests on extremely weak foundations and appears impossible to translate into reality."

In April 1492, Columbus renewed his appeal. This time, he was successful. Ferdinand and Isabella signed two "capitulations," or agreements. These documents detailed what royal support Columbus would receive. They also described the rewards he could expect if his mission was successful. The rulers promised to "appoint the said Christopher Columbus their Admiral in those Islands and Mainlands which by his labor and industry shall be discovered or acquired in the said Ocean Seas during his life." He would also be appointed governor of any lands he discovered. These rights would be passed on to his heirs at the time of his death. After Columbus paid back the money he borrowed, Columbus would also receive one-tenth of any profits from the trip. The rest would belong to the Spanish crown.

Columbus was given two caravels, the *Pinta* and the *Niña*. The two ships were captained by two brothers, Martín Alonso Pinzón and Vicente Yáñez Pinzón. For his flagship, Columbus chartered a larger ship, the *Santa Maria*. It was owned and commanded by Juan de la Cosa. All but four of the 90 officers, sailors, and apprentices in the fleet were Spaniards.

FIRST VOYAGE

Columbus's tiny fleet set sail from Palos, in southern Spain, on August 3, 1492. After pausing to pick up supplies in the Canary Islands, they headed into unfamiliar Atlantic waters on September 6. Most sea voyages of the era were relatively short. As the days at sea became weeks, Columbus's crewmen became uneasy. He began to keep two logbooks. In one, he overestimated the expedition's progress to calm the nerves of the crew. In the other logbook, he secretly recorded their actual progress. The ships and their restless sailors passed far beyond the point at which Columbus had calculated they would land at Japan. They were somewhat heartened by signs that land must be somewhere within reach when migrating birds passed overhead. Objects like leaves and tree branches floated past.

On the night of October 11, a light was briefly sighted in the distance. The men's hearts sank when it disappeared. It had been more than a month since they left the Canary Islands. At 2 A.M., sailor Rodrigo de Triana sighted a distant small island and shouted out the news.

At daylight, Columbus and the other captains went ashore. Columbus claimed the land for Spain. Inhabitants of the island, who did not understand Columbus's declaration that they were now Spanish subjects, gathered on the beach. The first awkward communication between Europeans and the people of the Americas began. Columbus offered trinkets such as beads, hawks' bells, and red caps. The islanders replied with gifts of "skeins of spun cotton, and parrots, and darts." They told the Spaniards that their island was called Guanahaní. Columbus gave it the name San Salvador (Holy Savior).

The people of the island were Arawak-speaking Taino. All were "naked as their mothers bore them," Columbus wrote. Some wore ornamental body paint. Others showed battle scars. Columbus asked in sign language about the wounds. The Taino replied that the scars were the result of fighting off slaving raids from neighboring islands. Trying to please his royal sponsors, Columbus wrote:

> They ought to be good servants and of good skill, for I see that they repeat very quickly what was said to them. I believe that they would easily be made Christians, because it seemed to me that they belonged to no religion. I, please Our Lord, will carry off six of them at my departure to your Highnesses, that they may learn to speak [Spanish].

Although Columbus had not reached a wealthy Asian empire, he noticed the Taino custom of wearing small gold nose pendants. Upon leaving Guanahaní, Columbus determined to search for gold. He planned his route accordingly.

> [T]hose whom I captured on the Island of San Salvador told me that there they wore very big bracelets of gold on their legs and arms. I well believed that all they said was humbug in order to escape. However, it was my wish to bypass no island without taking possession.

Despite having kidnapped his Taino guides, relations between Columbus's expedition and the people of each Bahamian island he visited were friendly. The Taino told Columbus of a large island they called "Colba." From their descriptions, Columbus was sure that it must be Japan. In fact, it was the island of Cuba. He set sail in its direction. The expedition did not find Asians or much gold when it reached Cuba. The Europeans who went ashore did notice Taino men and women inhaling smoke from lit bundles of herbs, called tobaccos. This custom of smoking tobacco was then unknown outside of the Americas. It later spread throughout the world.

Their arrival in Cuba marked the first of many future challenges to Columbus's leadership. Martín Alonso Pinzón, the captain of the *Pinta*, learned that gold might be found on an island to the east. He disappeared with his ship, without informing Columbus. The remaining ships sailed southeast along Cuba's coast. Because of its size, Columbus concluded that Cuba was not an island but a peninsula attached to China, somewhere to the west. Deciding that he would return in the future to explore this theory, he continued east. He reached the island that would one day be divided into the countries of Haiti and the Dominican Republic. He named it La Isla Española (The Spanish Island). It is known today as Hispaniola.

Columbus considered Hispaniola to be the most beautiful and peaceful of the islands he had yet seen. "In all the world, there can be no better or gentler people," he wrote of its inhabitants. They also wore plentiful gold jewelry. Near the present-day northern Haitian city of Cap Haitien, Columbus received an invitation to visit a cacique, or tribal leader, named Guacanagarí. Guacanagarí's lands were called Cibao. Columbus mistook that for Marco Polo's name for Japan, Cipangu. Certain that he had at last reached his goal, Columbus ordered the *Santa Maria* and the *Niña* to sail along the coast to meet Guacanagarí. On Christmas 1492, disaster struck.

That night, against orders, an exhausted sailor handed the *Santa Maria*'s steering tiller over to an inexperienced ship's boy. He let the ship drift onto a reef. Coral tore through the ship's planking and seawater filled the *Santa Maria*. With help from the locals, Columbus's men were able to unload all of their supplies and get ashore.

Columbus decided that the wrecking of the *Santa Maria* was a sign from God that he should found a colony in Hispaniola. He recruited 39 volunteers and told them to build a base from which to search for gold. The colony would be called Villa de la Navidad (Town of the Nativity).

The *Niña* sailed for Spain on January 4, 1493. Two days later, the *Pinta* caught up with it. Its crew told of having found gold in the countryside of Hispaniola. The two ships sailed together across the Atlantic Ocean until mid-February. A storm separated them, so they docked briefly in the Azores (a chain of islands about 930 miles, or 1,500 km, from Lisbon). Next they crossed violent seas all the way to the European mainland. Columbus and the *Niña* safely reached Portugal on March 4. Columbus wrote to João II, the Portuguese king, hoping the king would provide safe passage to Spain. The king invited the explorer to visit him at his summer home nearby.

João II had rejected Columbus's appeal for help eight years earlier. He suspected that Columbus had not visited new lands. Instead, he thought, Columbus had been meddling in Portuguese territory in Africa. Columbus's captive Taino interpreters convinced João II that Columbus told the truth. The king ignored advice to have him killed, which would prevent Spain from profiting from the discovery. Instead, he allowed Columbus to travel on. Columbus sent word to the Spanish rulers that he was on his way. He returned to Spain aboard the *Niña* on March 15. Amazingly, the *Pinta* sailed into the harbor the same afternoon. Columbus's greeting by the royal court at Barcelona was his greatest moment of triumph. He was awarded all the honors promised by Spanish royalty. Unfortunately, he spent the rest of his life fighting to hold on to those rewards.

SECOND VOYAGE

Columbus set sail on his second voyage from Cadiz (in southwestern Spain) on September 25, 1493. He still planned to reach China, but he had other goals, too. Colonization and religious conversion were now important.

In contrast to the fleet on his first voyage, his second fleet was huge. It included three large ships, 14 caravels, and 1,500 men. The Taino he had kidnapped had learned to speak Spanish. One remained at the Spanish court while the rest sailed back to the Caribbean.

On November 3, the fleet sighted islands in the chain that became known as the Lesser Antilles. Naming the islands as he progressed, Columbus followed the islands northwest to St. Croix, the Virgin Islands, and Puerto Rico. On November 27, he arrived at La Navidad, the outpost he had left on Hispaniola. No one was there. Columbus learned that the Taino had lost patience with the settlers' incessant demands for gold and women and had killed them all.

Columbus sailed east along the coast. He made a second attempt at founding a trading colony near present-day Puerto Plata, on the north-central coast of the Dominican Republic. He named it La Isabela, in honor of Spain's queen. Columbus left his inexperienced brother Diego in command of the colony. He then marched into the interior of the island, looking for a major source of gold. When he returned, he found the settlers of Isabela at the point of mutiny. After restoring order by

During his second voyage, Columbus came back to La Navidad (present-day Haiti) to find that the settlement had been destroyed and his men had been murdered by the Taino (*depicted above*).

force, Columbus set sail again in April 1494. He was certain that he could discover the Chinese mainland.

Columbus remained convinced that Cuba was a Chinese peninsula. He returned to the island's southern coast, sailing against the wind almost all the way to the island's western tip. If Columbus had continued 50 more miles (80 km), Cuba's true shape would have become clear. Instead, he halted the westward voyage and declared that Cuba was China. He ordered his crew to swear to an oath that they had found China. He warned that they would have their tongues cut out if they should ever break their oaths.

By early 1495, Columbus was more occupied with calming colonial discontent than with discovery. He tried to calm the Spanish gentlemen who had traveled with him to Hispaniola. They expected to find a comfortable, exotic haven with an unlimited supply of gold. Instead, they found themselves suffering in tropical rain. They went hungry rather

DISEASE IN THE NEW WORLD

Disease was the most destructive force arriving in the Americas with Europeans. The deadly diseases included smallpox, diphtheria, whooping cough, influenza, tuberculosis, pneumonia, mumps, and measles. Europeans had developed some natural resistance to these illnesses. The inhabitants of the Americas, however, had never been exposed to these potentially fatal diseases. Many became sick and died. More indigenous people died from disease than from forced labor and war combined.

One disease that may have moved in the other direction is syphilis. Europeans became aware of syphilis only in the mid-1490s. Some scientists continue to debate whether syphilis existed in the Old World before 1492 or whether it was first imported to Europe by Columbus's crew or the Taino captives his first voyage brought to Barcelona. Similarly, scientists continue to examine the origins of malaria and yellow fever. These mosquito-borne diseases probably came to the Americas from Africa after African slaves arrived in the early 1500s.

than eat the unfamiliar food of "the Indies." Instead of farming or pros-pecting, the Spanish pressed the native peoples for food and more gold. Resentment turned into open rebellion. The Arawak tribes resisted their demands. Forced labor and disease began to kill the native inhabitants of Hispaniola in large numbers. This pattern spread throughout the region as more colonists arrived.

Leaving his brothers Diego and Bartolomé in charge, Columbus sailed for Spain on March 10, 1496. Meanwhile, news of colonial dis-content and Columbus's harsh treatment of the Native Peoples had reached the Spanish court. The king and queen began to question his leadership.

COLUMBUS'S THIRD VOYAGE

Unlike later explorers, who relied on investors speculating on the discov-ery of gold or other wealth, Columbus continued to rely on royal backing for his voyages. Unable to present the Spanish court with grand success, he was in constant fear that each voyage would be his last. Columbus sailed west with six ships on May 30, 1498. He hoped to find enough riches to convince the king and queen that his voyages were worthwhile.

This time Columbus took a southerly route. He crossed the Atlantic Ocean close to the equator. Past the Canary Islands, he sent three ships ahead to Hispaniola. He hoped the other three would find the mainland of Asia. The heat of the southerly route ruined food and wine. Father Bartolomé de Las Casas wrote that "the heat was so intense and scorch-ing that they were afraid the men and ships would burn up."

The ships eventually picked up speed and crossed the Atlantic. They first sighted an island with three mountain peaks. Columbus named the island Trinidad, after the Holy Trinity. The ships rounded the southwest corner of Trinidad. Just then, they were struck by a terrifying tidal or volcanic disturbance. The channel is still known by the name Columbus gave it—Boca del Sierpe, the Serpent's Mouth. A short sail directly north took the ships to the tip of the Paria Peninsula, on the eastern coast of what is now Venezuela. On August 5, Columbus landed there. He was the first European explorer to set foot on the South American mainland.

Columbus assumed Paria was an island and named it Isla de García. A year later, Alfonso de Ojeda's expedition would name the same land Venezuela. Columbus next headed north to Hispaniola. He found his brothers fighting a group of rebellious colonists. Ferdinand and Isabella became convinced that their admiral could not govern. They dispatched a new governor, Francisco de Bobadilla, to Hispaniola. He was given power to investigate and end any rebellion. Bobadilla arrived at Santo Domingo in Hispaniola on August 23, 1500. When Columbus refused to accept the royal document appointing Bobadilla, the new governor had all three Columbus brothers arrested. They were chained and shipped back to Spain. The Spanish rulers were shocked by Columbus's humiliation. They ordered him freed and his property restored, but his role as governor of the Indies was over.

COLUMBUS'S FINAL VOYAGE

By 1502, Columbus's reputation was in tatters. The Spanish rulers nevertheless agreed to fund Columbus's final voyage. Columbus remembered Marco Polo's account of voyaging westward through the South China Sea. He was still convinced that Cuba was part of China and hoped to find a strait connecting the Caribbean to the Indian Ocean.

He set sail from Cadiz on May 11, 1502, with four ships. His 13-year-old son and future biographer, Ferdinand, joined him. The fleet crossed the Atlantic swiftly, discovering the island of Martinique along the way. To avoid any political problems, the Spanish rulers had ordered Columbus not to land at Hispaniola. Using the excuse that a storm was approaching, Columbus sailed into the harbor of Santo Domingo. The new governor, Nicolás Ovando, refused him permission to land. Columbus sailed on to a harbor just west of the colony and sheltered there from the storm he had predicted.

After reaching Cuba by way of Jamaica, Columbus sailed westward. He searched for the strait that would lead him to the Indian Ocean. Other explorers had by now explored the coast of South America between the Orinoco River and Panama. The rest of the Gulf of Mexico lay unexplored and open to the theory that such a connecting channel to India existed.

Instead of finding China, Columbus found himself off the coast of Honduras. After a month of struggling against winds, he turned south. He sailed along the coasts of present-day Nicaragua and Costa Rica. Columbus was sick for much of the voyage. By autumn 1502, he realized that he would not find a route to China. Instead, he bartered for gold with the Native Peoples. He also searched for a site to establish a

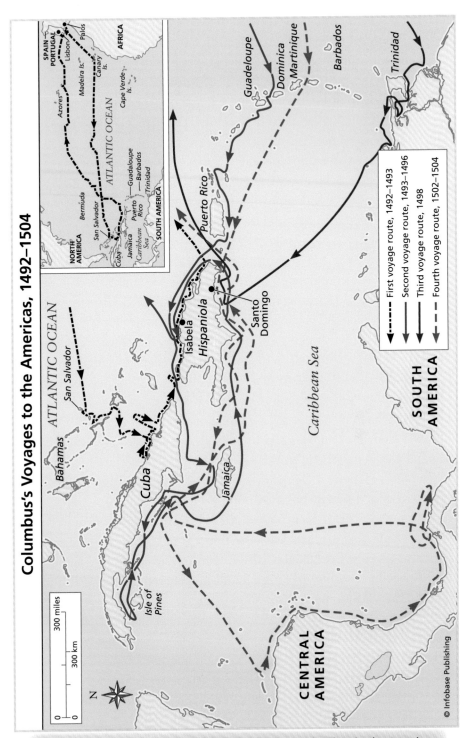

Columbus's Voyages to the Americas, 1492–1504

First voyage route, 1492–1493
Second voyage route, 1493–1496
Third voyage route, 1498
Fourth voyage route, 1502–1504

SPAIN
PORTUGAL
Lisbon
Palos
AFRICA
Madeira Is.
Azores
Canary Is.
Cape Verde Is.
ATLANTIC OCEAN
Bermuda
NORTH AMERICA
San Salvador
Cuba
Jamaica
Caribbean Sea
Puerto Rico
Guadeloupe
Barbados
Trinidad
SOUTH AMERICA

ATLANTIC OCEAN
Bahamas
San Salvador
Cuba
Isle of Pines
Isabela
Hispaniola
Santo Domingo
Jamaica
Caribbean Sea
Puerto Rico
Guadeloupe
Dominica
Martinique
Barbados
Trinidad
SOUTH AMERICA
CENTRAL AMERICA

N
300 miles
300 km

© Infobase Publishing

This map shows the four voyages of Christopher Columbus in the Americas, as well as his route across the Atlantic Ocean.

trading outpost. In January 1503, he picked a location near the mouth of the Río Belén in rugged northwestern Panama. By spring, however, relations with the area's Guaymi inhabitants had deteriorated so badly that Columbus's party was attacked. The Spaniards were forced to abandon one of their ships. They sailed for home on April 16. "I departed," Columbus wrote, "in the name of the Holy Trinity, on Easter night, with ships rotten, worn out, and eaten into holes."

None of the three ships made it to Spain. One was abandoned at the harbor of Puerto Bello in central Panama. The other two tried to reach Hispaniola but were leaking badly. They got as far as Jamaica. Columbus ordered them run aground on the beaches at St. Ann's Bay, on the northern coast.

The ships were too seriously damaged to be repaired. Columbus ordered a canoe commanded by Diego Méndez to make the 108-mile (173.8-km) trip to Hispaniola for help. Méndez reached Hispaniola, but Governor Ovando did not send a rescue ship to Jamaica for a year. Most of the survivors then remained in Hispaniola to try their luck as colonists, while Columbus continued on to Spain. He arrived in November 1504.

Columbus had failed to discover a route to China. He had also failed to return with anything of material worth. By now, years of stress and illness had taken their toll on him. On November 26, 1504, Queen Isabella died. She had been Columbus's supporter. Although King Ferdinand was sympathetic to the ailing admiral's condition, he refused Columbus's requests to be reappointed governor of the Indies. Still trying to reclaim his former glory, Columbus died on May 20, 1506.

Columbus's death went unnoticed by the Spanish public and royalty. He had failed to reach Asia or to find a grand treasure. He also had failed to manage his colonies. These failures had made him unpopular, especially as other explorers found greater sources of wealth and pushed deeper into newly discovered lands.

Despite these failures, Columbus's voyages opened a new age of discovery. For many of the native societies he and his successors encountered, the coming changes would be tragic. Columbus's encounters with the Americas immediately and permanently altered the course of history. They forced people on both sides of the Atlantic Ocean to view their world differently.

3

A New World
1500–1519

NOT LONG AFTER COLUMBUS'S FIRST VOYAGE, OTHER EXPLORERS sailed for the New World. At first, they, too, believed that the land they were exploring was part of Asia. While most searched for gold, pearls, and slaves, they also continued to hunt for a route to Asia. They were prevented by treaty from reaching Asia by sailing around Africa. Called the Treaty of Tordesillas, this agreement divided the "newly discovered" lands outside Europe between Spain and Portugal. The line of demarcation was about halfway between the Cape Verde Islands (already Portuguese) and the islands discovered by Columbus on his first voyage (Cuba and Hispaniola, which were claimed by Spain). Portugal took control of the east, while Spain had the lands to the west.

IN COLUMBUS'S WAKE

On Spain's side of the line demarcated by the Treaty of Tordesillas, fortune-seeking explorers began to sail along the northern coastline of South America. Unlike Columbus, whose voyages were financed by the Spanish crown, new explorers were required to pay their own way or find investors. Their geographical knowledge grew as mariners examined one another's charts. Their findings gradually reached cartographers in Europe.

Few of them found the new lands profitable enough to remain there for long. Vicente Yáñez Pinzón, who had served as captain of Columbus's caravel the *Niña*, sighted Brazil in 1500 but the land was claimed on April 22 of that year by Pedro Álvares Cabral on behalf of Portugal. When he crossed the Atlantic to South America, Cabral went so far west that he sailed to the mouth of the Rio Buranhém in present-day Bahia, a coastal state in Brazil. He considered the new land only a diversion from his real goal of reaching India. His ships explored the coast for just nine days, naming the land Isle de Vera Cruz. European settlers that came after named it Brazil.

Amerigo Vespucci was born in Florence, Italy, but worked in Seville, Spain, as an agent of the powerful Florentine Medici family. He made at least two and perhaps four voyages to the New World. His first voyage took place in about 1497–1498. He sailed north from Brazil to the east coast of North America. He may have reached Cape Hatteras, North Carolina, or even the Gulf of St. Lawrence. The only account of the trip

Amerigo Vespucci is credited with completing at least two transatlantic trips to the Americas. Vespucci found that the landmasses they explored were much larger than anticipated and different than described by earlier explorers. He concluded that this must be a new continent, not the eastern part of Asia, as Columbus believed.

appears in one of Vespucci's letters. Its lack of detail makes his claim controversial. If true, then Vespucci landed on the mainland of the Americas before Columbus.

Sailing for Portugal in 1501, Vespucci returned to Brazil and continued sailing south. It is unknown how far south he reached. This voyage convinced many Europeans that the Western Hemisphere was indeed a "New World," not part of Asia.

Vespucci returned to Spain, where he was appointed "pilot major," or chief navigator, by King Ferdinand. He spent the rest of his life serving in this important post. He was responsible for training and licensing pilots, preparing maps, and collecting information from sea captains returning from the New World.

Vasco Núñez de Balboa sailed from Spain in 1501. He settled on the island of Hispaniola and became a planter, but by 1510 he was broke. To escape his creditors, he hid inside a barrel aboard a ship bound for the eastern shore of the Gulf of Urabá, on the northern coast of South America. When the ship landed, the colonists were in danger of perishing from starvation and Native American attacks. Its leader, Martín de Enciso, accepted the stowaway's advice to move the group to a Native American village on the gulf's western shore, which Balboa had spotted on an earlier voyage. The new colony was named Santa María la Antigua de Darién (now known as Panama). Balboa soon became its leader.

Balboa married the daughter of an indigenous leader named Chima. He helped Chima's people fight a war against their enemies. Chima's people gave gold to the Spaniards for their help. An argument broke out among the Spaniards over how much gold to send to the king of Spain. One indigenous prince was disgusted. "I will show you a region flowing with gold," he said, "where you may satisfy your ravening appetites." This region, the Spaniards were told, lay to the west on the other side of the mountains of central Panama. From there, a large sea could be seen.

Hoping to prove his worth to the king as colonial leader, in 1512 Balboa led a small expedition into the southwest corner of Colombia looking for gold. He found little more than cinnamon trees, but he was the first European to see the Andes Mountains. On his return to Panama, when it seemed likely that he might be sent to Spain under arrest, Balboa organized another expedition. He was in search of riches that would make the colony a success.

On September 1, 1513, Native American guides led 190 Spaniards and hundreds of Native American porters into the mountains. They had to hack their way through the jungle. Throughout his progress across the Isthmus of Panama, Balboa offered peaceful alliances to friendly Native Peoples and violently conquered any who resisted him. The expedition struggled for three weeks through swamps and over mountains that remain barely accessible even today.

Balboa was the first European to see the Pacific Ocean from the west. On the morning of September 27, he walked ahead of his men to the top of a hill. He suddenly spotted the vast waters, which he called Mar del

NAMING AMERICA

Martin Waldseemüller, a cartographer and geographer, accepted Amerigo Vespucci's claims that he had reached a new continent. In 1507, he published and sold 1,000 copies of a large woodcut map. It was called "Map of the World According to the Traditions of Ptolemy and Americus Vespucius."

The map showed the Caribbean and the eastern coastlines of the Western Hemisphere as separate from Asia. It strengthened the idea that these lands belonged to a "New World." They were not part of China as Columbus and others had hoped. Waldseemüller showed the northern and southern continents separately. The southern portion is now called South America. On it, Waldseemüller drew a large portrait of Amerigo Vespucci. Waldseemüller suggested in a book that "since another . . . part [of the world] has been discovered by Americus Vesputius, I do not see why anyone should object to its being called after Americus the Discoverer, a man of natural wisdom, Land of Americus or America."

Waldseemüller stopped using the name America in his later maps, perhaps to correct his mistake of giving Vespucci so much credit. By then, however, the 1507 map was used throughout Europe. The matter was unofficially decided in 1538. That year, Belgian cartographer Gerard Mercator published a map dividing the New World into "North America" and "South America."

Sur, the "Sea of the South." Four days later, the men reached the Pacific Ocean. Balboa claimed the sea and all the contiguous lands for Spain.

On January 18, 1514, Balboa arrived back in Darién. He had not lost a single member of his expedition. Unfortunately for Balboa, King Ferdinand had sent a new governor to the colony, a ruthless nobleman named Pedro Arias de Ávila. He arrived with 2,000 settlers and soldiers, who were dismayed to discover that the grand city they expected was little more than a frontier settlement. Balboa busied himself by transporting shipbuilding materials to the Pacific coast. Two ships were built. They reached the Pearl Islands in the Gulf of Panama in 1517; however, Balboa's attempts to sail southward were stopped by rough weather. The new governor lured Balboa back to Darién and charged him with treason and other crimes. After a long series of trials on false charges, Balboa was beheaded on January 21, 1519.

PONCE DE LEÓN AND "LA FLORIDA"

Juan Ponce de León was a veteran of Columbus's second voyage. He had fought in the conquests of Hispaniola and Puerto Rico. After serving as Puerto Rico's governor and becoming rich with gold mined by indigenous slave labor, Ponce got permission from King Ferdinand to search for and settle the "Island of Bimini." This land was thought to have a "fountain of youth." The expedition was funded at Ponce de León's expense, not the crown's.

Ponce sailed from Puerto Rico in March 1513 with three ships. The route took them past the eastern limits of the Bahamas, sailing northwest. On April 2, members of the fleet thought they had found the island. Because they arrived in the Easter season, which was called La Pascua Florida, Ponce named it La Florida. They landed just south of present-day Daytona Beach, on Florida's northeastern coast at a location known today as Ponce de León Inlet.

Ponce sailed south. His expedition became the first Europeans to encounter the Gulf Stream, one of the strongest ocean currents in the world. He stopped at Native American villages, each time asking about the "fountain of youth." He passed the Florida Keys, then turned north into the Gulf of Mexico. The ships anchored in Charlotte Bay, a third of the way up the Florida peninsula's west coast. Friendly relations with the Calusa Indians quickly deteriorated into open warfare. On June 14, Ponce ordered a return to Puerto Rico.

Less than two weeks after leaving Florida, the crews sighted land and briefly went ashore. They thought it was Cuba. It may have been the coast of Mexico. They were perhaps the first Europeans to step foot on Mexico.

Ponce de León met a violent end. In 1521, he equipped a large expedition for settlement and sailed for Florida. Upon landing, however, he encountered the same tribe with which he had clashed earlier, the Calusa. They fought, and Ponce was wounded in the thigh by an arrow. He was taken to Cuba, where the infected wound killed him. His death left the European exploration and settlement of Florida to later adventurers.

"NEW SPAIN"

Only 25 years after Columbus's first arrival in the Americas, diseases, warfare, and slavery had killed much of the Native population. Thousands, possibly millions, of Native Peoples died working in Spanish mines and from illnesses common in Europe. Spain's governor of Cuba, Diego Velásquez, faced a shrinking slave workforce. Yet, settlers from Spain continued to arrive. Velásquez promised them workers "as soon as there were any to spare."

Díaz del Castillo was tired of Velásquez's promises. He and others decided to "try our fortune in seeking and exploring new lands where we might find employment." The group appointed Francisco Hernández de Córdoba as their leader and bought three ships, including one from Velásquez.

They sailed westward from Cuba in February 1517. Three weeks later they sighted the Yucatán Peninsula at Cape Catoche. This was the land of the great Maya civilization which had declined 500 years before Córdoba arrived. The Spaniards saw the great Mayan temples and gold ornaments. They were convinced that they had stumbled upon a land full of riches.

The Spaniards sailed along the west coast of Yucatán, which they mistook for an island. Mayan soldiers fought them each time they tried to land. The men were desperately in need of drinking water, so they decided to sail for Florida. Unfortunately, the ships landed at the same spot where Ponce de León had clashed with the Calusa. They, too, attacked as soon as the Spaniards landed. The ships limped to Cuba. Like Ponce de León, Córdoba died of wounds he sustained in Florida.

Governor Velásquez sent a stronger expedition to Yucatán in 1518. It was under the command of Juan de Grijalva. He named the land "New Spain," a term later applied to all of Mexico. When Grijalva returned to the site where Córdoba had landed, he, too, was attacked. Grijalva, however, convinced the Mayan that he wanted to trade peacefully. The Spaniards were delighted to trade colored glass beads for food, textiles—and gold. The Spaniards asked for more gold. The Mayan replied that "further on, in the direction of the sunset, there was plenty of gold." The land, they said, was called Mexico. This would become the next goal of the Spanish.

CORTÉS THE EXPLORER

Cuba's governor, Diego Velásquez, acted quickly. He ordered Hernán Cortés to find this land of gold. Cortés's popularity as mayor of the Cuban town of San Juan de Baracoa helped him enlist volunteers and investors for his expedition. He was forced to leave Cuba in secret after learning that Velásquez had become suspicious and intended to revoke his support of the venture. Cortés sailed on February 10, 1519, with 11 ships, 508 men, and 16 horses. The expedition reached the island of Cozumel, 12 miles (19 km) off the Yucatán Peninsula. One of its first objectives was to find an interpreter. Incredibly, for a small ransom, the local people produced a Maya-speaking Spanish priest. Jerónimo de Aguilar had been shipwrecked on the Mexican mainland eight years earlier.

Cortés's ships continued west along the gulf coast. They anchored on March 12, 1519, near the town of Tabasco. Thousands of armed Mayan were waiting on the shore. Cortés declared that he wished to trade, but the Tabascans refused. Cortés ignored their warnings not to land and fought his way into town, claiming the land for King Charles V. After several days of battle, the Tabascans pleaded for peace. They presented Cortés with gifts, including 20 female slaves. One of these young women was known as "Malinche." The Spaniards baptized her with the Christian name Doña Marina. She spoke both Maya and Nahuatl, the language of the Aztec. She learned Spanish so quickly that she became Cortés's translator and guide. Malinche was a valuable adviser to the Spanish conquerors. Later generations of Mexicans considered her a traitor to the nation.

MOCTEZUMA'S DILEMMA

The Spanish ships sailed northward. On Good Friday 1519, the ships dropped anchor in the harbor of the present-day city of Veracruz. Ambassadors of Aztec emperor Moctezuma II approached. The Aztecs had first learned of Spanish activities along the coast, ever since Hernández

When Moctezuma first heard about Hernán Cortés, the Aztec ruler thought the explorer was a god. Although Moctezuma was uncertain in his dealings with Cortés, he continued to be welcoming, even after Cortés took him prisoner.

de Córdoba's expedition two years earlier. The Spaniards were described as strangers who came from "great floating towers." Such news created confusion in Tenochtitlán, the Aztec capital. The Aztecs had already been unnerved by a series of disturbing omens and prophecies. One of these told of the destruction of their empire by foreigners.

Equally unsettling were descriptions of Spanish horses and weapons, which the Aztecs had never seen. "Their deer carry them on their backs wherever they wish to go," Moctezuma's ambassadors told their emperor. "Those deer, our lord, are as tall as the roof of a house." Reports described the Spanish cannon: "a thing like a ball of stone comes out of its entrails; it comes out shooting sparks and raining fire. The smoke that comes out with it has a pestilent odor, like that of rotten mud. This odor penetrates even to the brain and causes the greatest discomfort. If the cannon is aimed against a mountain, the mountain splits and cracks open."

With a huge army at his command, Moctezuma could have destroyed the strangers. Yet, the Spanish arrival resembled the story of Quetzalcoatl, the Aztec god. Quetzalcoatl was light-skinned and bearded, like the Spaniards. Stories told that he left Mexico by sea and would return. Moctezuma did not know whether he should kill the strangers or welcome them. He decided to stall them. His ambassadors returned to Cortés with gifts of gold and silver. They declared that Moctezuma felt it was unnecessary to meet with the Spaniards as they desired.

JOURNEY TO TENOCHTITLÁN

Velásquez had told Cortés only to explore and trade with any indigenous peoples he met. Cortés had no legal standing to conquer or settle any land. He was not supposed to negotiate with Aztec leaders or even present himself as a representative of King Charles V. Now convinced there were riches in the Mexican interior, Cortés's supporters spread a rumor that Velásquez had betrayed the Spanish king. The expedition elected Cortés as their new leader. Cortés established a town he named Villa Rica de Vera Cruz (the present-day city of Veracruz). He shipped the gold presented by Moctezuma's ambassadors directly to Spain, with a positive report to the king.

Cortés realized that the towns through which he passed were unhappy under Aztec rule. Cortés left a small force at Vera Cruz. He destroyed his remaining ships so that no one could leave. He then marched inland. Moctezuma continued to send ambassadors to Cortés. They promised "tribute would be paid in gold and silver" if the foreigners would leave Mexico. They gave Cortés gifts of golden necklaces. These gifts made the Spanish more determined than ever to march onward.

The Spanish soldiers descended into the Valley of Mexico. They were amazed at the sight of Tenochtitlán. It was surrounded by the salt water of Lake Texcoco. Broad, fortified causeways led into the city. "We were amazed and said it was like the enchantments told of in the legend of Amadis [hero of a Spanish story], on account of the great towers and cues and buildings rising from the water, and all built of masonry," wrote Díaz del Castillo. "Some of our soldiers even asked whether the things that we saw were not a dream?"

A thousand Aztec citizens and nobles welcomed the Spaniards. At the edge of the city, Moctezuma met Cortés. Cortés said, "We have come to your house in Mexico as friends. There is nothing to fear."

Cortés and his men were housed in Moctezuma's palace. They stole all the gold objects they found and melted them into bars. Although he was treated as an honored guest, Cortés forbid Moctezuma from leaving the palace. Moctezuma, still confused over how to respond to the mysterious strangers, did not resist.

Cortés wrote a description of Tenochtitlán for his king, Charles V:

> The city itself is as big as Seville or Córdoba. There is also one square twice as big as that of Salamanca, with arcades all around, where more than sixty thousand people come each day to buy and sell, and where every kind of merchandise produced in these lands is found; provisions as well as ornaments of gold and silver, lead, brass, copper, tin, stones, shells, bones, and feathers. They also sell lime, hewn and unhewn stone, adobe bricks, tiles, and cut and uncut woods of various kinds. There is a street where they sell game and birds of every species found in this land. . . . They sell honey, wax, and a syrup made from maize canes, which is as sweet and syrupy as that made from sugar cane. They also make syrup from a plant which in the islands is called maguey, which is much better than most syrups, and from this plant they also make sugar and wine, which they likewise sell.

Cortés sent out several exploratory expeditions to seek gold. Only one of these parties had success, but they had learned about the features of the Mexican terrain. Aztec nobles grew irritated with Spanish demands for more gold. After six months in the capital, Cortés learned that he also faced a threat from Diego Velásquez. The governor had sent Pánfilo de Narváez and 900 men to arrest Cortés. When Cortés heard of Narváez's landing, he immediately marched to the coast. He defeated Narváez and convinced most of the new men to join him in Tenochtitlán.

In the meantime, the captain left in command at Tenochtitlán, Pedro de Alvarado, had given a catastrophic order. The most important of Aztec festivals, the fiesta of Toxcatl, took place during Cortés's absence. As the Aztecs celebrated, Alvarado and his men attacked and killed hundreds of Aztec nobles. Enraged Aztec citizens hurried to the site of the killing. Alvarado retreated to the royal palace and chained Moctezuma, who urged his people to stop attacking the Spaniards and return to their homes. The Aztec people, however, had lost their respect for Moctezuma during his humiliating captivity. They ignored his pleas.

The streets were empty when Cortés returned to Tenochtitlán. As Cortés scolded Alvavado, Aztec forces surrounded the palace. Fighting began and the ensuing battle lasted for four days. Moctezuma died during the fighting, either the victim of stones thrown by an angry Aztec crowd or murdered by Cortés's order. The Spanish fled the city on the night of June 30, 1520. By the time Cortés fought his way to safety in Tlaxcalan territory, the losses numbered 450 Spaniards and all of the treasure his men had looted from Aztec palaces. Their retreat is known to this day in Mexico as the Noche Triste (Sorrowful Night).

THE CONQUERORS RETURN

The Aztecs began to repair their city and resumed their way of life after the departure of the Spanish. Yet, Tenochtitlán was soon ravaged by smallpox, a disease that had been unknown in Mexico before the arrival of the Narváez force. Cortés regrouped his forces and returned to Lake Texcoco the following spring. The Spaniards built ships equipped with cannons for a naval assault. They blocked Tenochtitlán's causeways and began a bloody siege that lasted 80 days. At first, Aztec soldiers beat

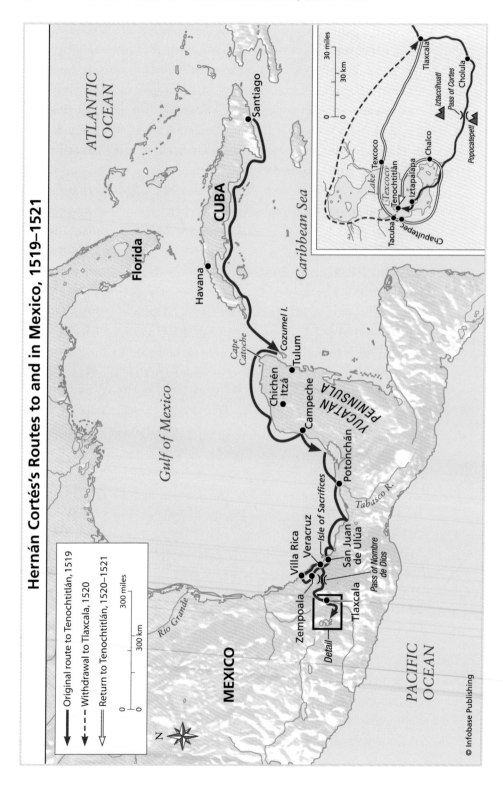

Hernán Cortés's Routes to and in Mexico, 1519–1521

— Original route to Tenochtitlán, 1519

---- Withdrawal to Tlaxcala, 1520

⇒ Return to Tenochtitlán, 1520–1521

© Infobase Publishing

back the Spanish. Smallpox, however, killed thousands of the starving Aztecs. Those that survived surrendered on August 13, 1521. More than half of the city's 300,000 defenders were dead. As the survivors were leaving the city, they were searched for treasure.

Cortés was appointed captain-general of New Spain on October 15, 1522. Rulers of many Mexican states agreed to become Spanish subjects. Others fought the Europeans to a standstill in Yucatán and other regions of Central America for decades.

Cortés sent out expeditions to survey the land. They reported on Mexico's natural resources. One of his main goals was to find a water route across this part of the Americas. He hoped it would connect the Atlantic and Pacific oceans. The water route was not found, yet the expeditions did discover much about the land's natural resources. They also found potential ports for Spanish ships along the Pacific coast. As a result, in 1523–1524, Pedro de Alvarado led an expedition down the Pacific coast to Honduras, while Cortés's nephew, Francisco Cortés, explored northward along the Pacific coast.

Cortés also faced problems with his own countrymen. One of his men, Cristóbal de Olid, proclaimed himself governor of Honduras. Cortés sent a fleet to defeat him. He soon received news that the ships were wrecked at sea. In 1524, Cortés led his own army toward Honduras. They were guided by little more than a compass and a map of Mayan traders' trails. At a treacherous mountain pass, 68 of the group's horses tumbled to their deaths. The rest were injured by the trail's jagged stones. When his force finally arrived in Honduras, they had been reduced by illness, starvation, and combat. Cortés found that Olid had been executed months earlier by survivors of the shipwrecked expedition. Then, he received even worse news. Cortés and his men were thought to have died in the jungles and their property in Mexico had been sold.

Cortés returned north to regain his leadership. His enemies had been busy in his absence. He was accused of falsely reporting the amount of

(opposite page) Just two years after entering Tenochtitlán, the capital city of the Aztec Empire, Cortés conquered its leader, Moctezuma, and the Aztec people. Cortés and his men looted the country of its treasures, claimed the country for Spain, and replaced the Aztec sacrificial altars with Christian ones.

treasure he had seized. He was also charged with plotting to become the ruler of Mexico. Cortés returned to Spain in December 1527 and cleared himself of all charges. He was named marquis of the Valley of Oaxaca and granted a huge estate within the land he had seized. He also obtained royal permission to organize expeditions in the Pacific Ocean.

CORTÉS AND CALIFORNIA

Cortés's history of disregarding authority made it possible for his Spanish enemies to convince the crown to limit his power in Mexico. The king forbade him to come within 25 miles (40 km) of Mexico City, as the Spanish settlement built on the ruins of Tenochtitlán was now called. Prevented from participating in colonial government, Cortés built an estate and researched plans for exploration from Mexico's west coast. For the first time, Cortés became a patron of discovery. He was content to let others explore on his behalf.

"They tell me that Ciguatan is an island inhabited by women," Cortés wrote to the Spanish king. "They also tell me it is very rich in pearls and gold, respecting which I shall labor to obtain the truth, and give your majesty a full account of it." The "island" of Ciguatan was actually the seaside town of Cihuatlan. This name was eventually turned into "California."

Cortés had three goals. The first was to find California. The second was to find a route to the Spice Islands. The third was to find a passage that linked the Pacific and Atlantic oceans. Nearly all the ventures ended in disaster. A 1532 expedition disappeared without a trace. Cortés sent ships in search of the expedition. The rescue group's commander was murdered in a mutiny.

These voyages were a financial disaster for Cortés. He returned to Spain in 1540 and died on December 2, 1547. By the time of Cortés's death, Spain was the main political power in Central America and Mexico. The Aztec Empire's grip on the peoples of Mexico had been destroyed, replaced by a system of Spanish influence and control.

Spain's foothold in the Western Hemisphere would shape the hemisphere's languages and cultural history. Cortés's discoveries confirmed Columbus's promise of wealth on the western shores of the Atlantic Ocean. It was finally clear that the Americas were a "New World." They were not part of Asia as Columbus had believed. With a major base, Europeans were about to flood onto the American mainland.

4

Pizarro, Peru, and South America 1531–1683

THE SPANISH WERE EXPLORERS AND CONQUERORS. SOME WERE more devoted to one role than the other. One who was more interested in conquering new lands than in exploring them was Francisco Pizarro. He was driven by a desire for wealth and power. At a terrible cost to Native Americans, he established the most significant base for the first wave of exploration—and exploitation—of South America.

PIZARRO'S EARLY EXPEDITIONS

Before his adventures in Peru, Pizarro was a retired soldier. He had marched to the Pacific Ocean with Vasco Núñez de Balboa in 1513. After Balboa's death, Pizarro remained in Panama. He became a mayor with a reputation for ruthlessness toward the Native Peoples. Pizarro heard rumors of wealth in the lands south of Panama and formed a partnership with another soldier, Diego de Almagro. A priest, Hernando de Luque, agreed to fund their expeditions.

Their first expeditions were failures. Pizarro's first voyage in 1524 down the west coast of Colombia was quickly halted by attacks by Native Americans and malaria. A second attempt took place from 1526–1527 and did only a little better, but it did result in an important discovery. Off the coast of Ecuador, the pilot, Bartolomé Ruiz, sighted a large oceangoing raft belonging to local peoples. Despite the excitement of the encounter, the expedition was soon on the edge of collapse again.

In April 1528, Pizarro and his crew sighted the Inca city of Tumbes on Peru's northwestern coast. Pizarro sent three men ashore

Francisco Pizarro explored the area of present-day Peru, then destroyed the Inca Empire. Pizarro arrived while the region was experiencing a civil war, giving him the opportunity to march through the Inca kingdom with limited resistance.

to investigate. The shore party returned with good news. They told of gold and silver, and friendly, intelligent men and beautiful women. The Spanish spent several weeks feasting and exchanging information with the locals. They enjoyed similar receptions at other coastal villages as far south as central Peru.

Pizarro returned to Panama, then quickly sailed for Spain. He was seeking investors and royal support. Its rulers authorized him to "discover" and conquer Peru. As soon as the conquest was complete, Peru would be called New Castile. Pizarro would govern it, an entitlement that his partner Almagro would object to later. From the start of his third and final expedition, Pizarro's goal was nothing less than complete possession of Peru.

THE FINAL EXPEDITION

Pizarro sailed to Peru from Panama in December 1530 with a small expedition. Only 180 men participated, including his half-brothers Hernando, Gonzalo, and Juan. They also included a cavalry company with 37 horses commanded by Hernando de Soto. When Pizarro reached Tumbes, he found Peru dramatically changed from what he had seen earlier.

Pizarro learned that Peru was near the end of a bloody four-year civil war. The Inca emperor Huayno Capac had died in 1528. His sons Huascar and Atahualpa both claimed to be the heir to the throne. Tens of thousands of people died in the fighting. When the Spanish arrived, Atahualpa was marching south. He hoped to complete his control of the empire by conquering its capital, Cuzco. With thousands of troops at his command, Atahualpa felt he had little to fear from a small group of Spanish soldiers.

Pizarro left Tumbes in May 1532. For months he marched inland, demanding the loyalty of local chiefs and gold. If they resisted, he killed them. In late 1532, Pizarro learned that Atahualpa was in northern Peru at Cajamarca. He was only 12 days' march away. The Spaniards hiked for a week over mountains nearly 14,000 feet (4,267 m) above sea level. On November 14, they saw Cajamarca in the valley below. It was surrounded by more than 30,000 of Atahualpa's soldiers.

Pizarro's cavalry captain Hernando de Soto rode to meet Atahualpa the next day. Atahualpa was scornful and unimpressed by the Spaniard. When Pizarro's brother Hernando joined them, Atahualpa announced that he had received reports of Spaniards enslaving his subjects. The Spaniards denied the charge. They claimed that 10 Spaniards would be enough to rid Atahualpa of his enemies. Atahualpa laughed. He agreed to meet Francisco Pizarro on the following day, November 16, 1532.

That night, Pizarro's men hid in the buildings surrounding Caja-marca's main square. The following afternoon, Atahualpa arrived. He was carried on a royal stretcher and accompanied by a large escort. Pizarro appeared and told Atahualpa that he was the friendly ambassa-dor of a great lord. A Peruvian historian, Felipe Guamán Poma de Ayala, described Atahualpa's reply:

> *The Inca responded with majesty and said that it was true that, having come as a messenger from so distant a land, he believed it must be a great lord, but that he did not have to make friendship, as he too was a great lord in his kingdom.*

Father Vicente Valverde, Pizarro's chaplain, told the emperor to renounce all gods except the one worshipped by the Spaniards. Ata-hualpa replied that he had to worship no gods but his own. He asked who had told the priest otherwise. Valverde responded that his Bible told him. Atahualpa demanded to see the book:

> *He took it in his hands and began to look through the pages of the book. And the Inca said: "Well, why doesn't it tell me? The book doesn't even talk to me!" Speaking with great majesty, seated in his throne, the Inca Atahualpa threw the book down from his hands.*

The angry priest shouted to Pizarro, who ordered the Spanish sol-diers to shoot. Concealed soldiers burst into the plaza. Atahualpa was seized unharmed, but between 2,000 and 10,000 unarmed Incas were killed in a slaughter that lasted for hours. The next morning, Pizarro ordered Atahualpa to command his army to disband. Most of the Inca troops left.

As Atahualpa watched the Spaniards pillage Cajamarca, he came up with a plan to save his own life. He drew a line high on a wall with a piece of chalk. He promised to fill the room to the mark once with gold and twice with silver if Pizarro would set him free. Pizarro immediately agreed. Collecting the ransom took the Spaniards deeper into Peru.

Atahualpa, the last Inca ruler, did not consider the small Spanish force to be a threat to his vast army. He invited Pizarro and his men to visit Cajamarca, with Atahualpa himself arriving dressed in ceremonial attire. Pizarro and his men ambushed the unsuspecting Inca army (*depicted above*) and captured Atahualpa.

Hernando Pizarro led a force south to Pachácamac and other Inca holy sites. He seized gold idols and melted them down.

In February 1533, Almagro arrived at Cajamarca with reinforcements. They immediately fought with Pizarro's men over division of the tons of gold and silver. By summer the ransom chamber was full. Pizarro, however, broke his promise. He accused Atahualpa of plotting against the Spaniards and ordering the murder of his brother Huascar. Atahualpa was killed on August 29, 1533.

Atahualpa's death allowed Pizarro to march throughout the Inca kingdom with limited opposition. In November 1533, the Spanish occupied the Inca capital of Cuzco. They also declared the Inca civil war to be over and appointed Manco Capac, brother of Huascar and Atahualpa, as the new ruler. The first year of Spanish control passed peacefully. In 1535, Pizarro founded the city of Lima a short distance from the coast. From there, he could manage outgoing treasure shipments.

Pizarro's governorship caused conflict with his business partners. The original agreement between Pizarro, Almagro, and Luque stated that the three would equally divide all their wealth. Pizarro's royal commission, however, placed control in his hands. Almagro was furious. Meanwhile, the first shipments of Peruvian treasure reached Spain, causing a flood of fortune seekers to travel to South America.

ALMAGRO IN CHILE

Almagro planned a new expedition. He wanted to explore lands that were rumored to hold even more wealth than the Inca Empire. He moved southeast into the great highland basin of southern Peru and western Bolivia. He followed the Desaguadero River toward the salt water of Lake Poopó. The countryside became increasingly bleak as Almagro continued south. He found little but deserts and desolate mountains.

Almagro entered the valleys of northern Argentina. He lost men in ambushes by Native American tribes unfamiliar even to the Inca. A large portion of his supplies was washed away in seasonal floods. Survival became more important than conquest. Almagro turned toward the Pacific coast, hoping to get supplies by sea. He divided his men into small groups and led them over deadly mountain ranges. Spanish historian Agustín del Zárate described the crossing:

> Many of those who had died remained, frozen solid, still on foot and propped against the rocks, and the horses they had been leading also frozen, not decomposed, but as fresh as if they had just died; and later expeditions following the same route, short of food, came upon these horses, and were glad to eat them.

Finding no treasure, Almagro realized his mission was a failure. To return to the Peruvian border, he first had to cross the 600-mile (955-km)-long Atacama Desert. Dividing into even smaller groups to conserve water, Almagro's men became the first Europeans to cross the Atacama.

Almagro's expedition arrived at Cuzco empty-handed in early 1537. They found the Pizarros fighting an Inca rebellion. The Spanish won the war within a year, however, armed resistance lasted another 35 years. By then, both Almagro and Francisco Pizarro were dead.

The two former partners had become enemies. Soon after Almagro's return from Chile, their supporters began fighting each other. Almagro's forces were defeated in 1538, and Pizarro had Almagro executed. Almagro's followers took revenge in 1541. They killed Francisco Pizarro in Lima.

ORELLANA AND THE AMAZON

While Francisco Pizarro lay dying, his brother Gonzalo was lost in the jungles east of the Andes. Gonzalo had been appointed governor of the areas that make up modern Ecuador. He had heard stories of the gold of El Dorado and abundant spices in La Canela, the "Land of Cinnamon."

Eager to surpass his brother's success, Gonzalo Pizarro had left Quito, in northern Ecuador, in February 1541. He led 220 soldiers and 4,000 chained indigenous slaves, who carried supplies. The expedition's progress soon slowed to a crawl due to the rainy season. The men hacked through roadless jungles. A month after setting forth, a company of cavalry reinforcements joined them. It was led by a one-eyed conquistador named Francisco Orellana.

Pizarro left his main army and set forth with 70 men. He wandered aimlessly in the "Land of Cinnamon." He discovered that it had little actual cinnamon. When he rejoined his main force two months later, most of his slaves were dead from disease and mistreatment. Many of the Spaniards had also died.

Pizarro struggled east along the River Coca, bearing the sick and remaining supplies on a hastily crafted boat. He forced his way 150 miles (241 km) eastward down the River Napo. Native American guides warned him that they were lost in a land with no food and far from any escape route back to the Andes. The day after Christmas 1541, with his starving men ready to mutiny, Pizarro agreed to let Orellana take the boat and 59 men downriver to seek food. Whether or not Pizarro ordered Orellana to return in a few days would later be disputed. Regardless, Orellana now commanded perhaps the greatest exploratory journey in South American history.

By his third day downriver, the current was too strong for Orellana to return to Pizarro's main force. A Dominican priest, Gaspar de Carvajal, described what happened in his memoirs:

We soon realized it was impossible to go back. We talked over our situation (seeing we were already nearly dead from hunger) and we chose what seemed to us the lesser of two evils . . . trusting to God to get us out, to go on and follow the river: we would either die or get to see what lay along it.

Five days into their journey, Orellana's men came upon a friendly Native American village. They rested there for a month, preparing for their voyage downriver into the unknown. Unlike the Pizarros, who would

THE LEGEND OF EL DORADO

Indian tales told of a man covered with gold. He was El Dorado ("the golden one"). In the legend, an ancient coronation ritual took place at Lake Guatavita, just north of Bogotá. The new ruler, religious leaders, and a heap of gold were floated aboard a raft into the lake. There the new ruler would be covered with mud and gold dust. Then the men threw piles of gold into the lake. There the new ruler would be:

stripped to his skin, and anointed with a sticky earth on which they placed the gold dust so that he was completely covered with this metal . . . when they reached the centre of the lagoon . . . the gilded Indian made his offering, throwing out all the pile of gold into the middle of the lake, and the chiefs accompanying him did the same.

Gold-hungry conquistadores believed that the lake was filled with treasure. In 1545, Gonzalo Jiménez de Quesada partially drained the lake and found 4,000 gold coins. Later attempts, which continued for centuries, produced mostly mud.

Over time, the term *El Dorado* came to refer to an entire golden city instead of one man. Similar legends spread throughout the Americas and encouraged illusions such as the Seven Cities of Cíbola, which was sought by Spanish conquistador Francisco Vásquez de Coronado. Although never found, El Dorado's grip on the imagination spurred exploration throughout the Americas for decades.

torture Native Americans to get information, Orellana tried to learn their language. "Next to God," Father Carvajal would write, "the captain's ability to speak the languages of the natives was the thing that saved our lives."

Ten days after resuming his voyage, Orellana came to where the Napo met the Marañón River to form one great river. From this point, which he called St. Eulalia, the men moved down the river more than 2,000 miles (3,218 km) later. This river was later named Río Amazonas, the River of the Amazons.

The leader of several local villages was named Aparia. The Spaniards lived with Aparia's people for two months. The Aparians warned of two hostile Native American states downriver. The states were named after their rulers, Machiparo and Omagua.

The Spaniards were attacked repeatedly as they drifted hundreds of miles past the villages of Machiparo and Omagua. They went ashore whenever they could. They discovered fields of fruit trees and broad roads leading into the countryside.

Throughout their journey, Orellana and his men had heard stories of a tribe of warrior women, called Amazons. The Amazons were a mythical tribe of Greek female warriors. Constant attacks by Native Americans resumed as the Spaniards came closer to the coast. On June 24, 1542, Carvajal wrote:

> Here we came suddenly upon the excellent land and dominion of the Amazons. These said villages had been forewarned and knew of our coming, in consequence thereof they came out on the water to meet us, in no friendly mood, and, when they had come close to the Captain [Orellana], he would have liked to induce them to accept peace . . . but they laughed, and mocked us and told us to keep going and that down below they were waiting for us, and that they were to seize us all and take us to the Amazons.

Orellana's men were soon battling a large force of "Amazons," whose ranks, according to Carvajal, contained a dozen women:

> These women are very white and tall, and have hair very long and braided and wound about the head, and they are very robust and go about naked, with their privy parts covered, with their bows

and arrows in their hands, doing as much fighting as ten Indian men, and indeed there was one Indian woman among these who shot an arrow a span deep into one of our brigantines, and others less deep, so that our brigantines looked like porcupines.

A few days after fighting the "Amazons," Orellana's men realized they were near an ocean. They were close to starvation. They landed and did their best to make their crude boats seaworthy. On August 26, 1542, they sailed into the Atlantic.

They were 1,200 miles (1,931 km) from Spanish settlements. They had two small boats, which they sailed north along the Brazilian coast. They were always in danger of being destroyed by ocean seas. After a storm separated the boats, each crew assumed the other was lost. After rounding Trinidad, they were reunited on September 11, 1542, at Cubagua, off the Venezuelan coast. They had reached a colony of Spanish pearl extractors.

During Orellana's amazing journey, Gonzalo Pizarro managed to return to Peru. His horrendous ordeal took the lives of all but 80 of his men. Pizarro was astonished and infuriated to learn that Orellana was alive. He was even angrier upon learning of his brother Francisco's murder.

Pizarro fought to regain control of Peru. The conquistador met his end when he led a revolt of colonists against the Spanish crown's new laws restricting the rights of conquistadores and protecting the rights of indigenous peoples. He was executed in 1548, only seven years after his brother's assassination.

Orellana convinced the Spanish court that his trip down the Amazon had not resulted from a mutiny. He was ordered to conquer the regions he had discovered. He collected a force of 400 men. With his young wife aboard, they sailed west. They reached Brazil around Christmas 1545

(opposite page) Conquistadores traveled to the Americas to spread their religion and to "bring civilization" to the indigenous peoples. The Spanish quickly took control of places like Peru and Chile, changing the face of South America altogether.

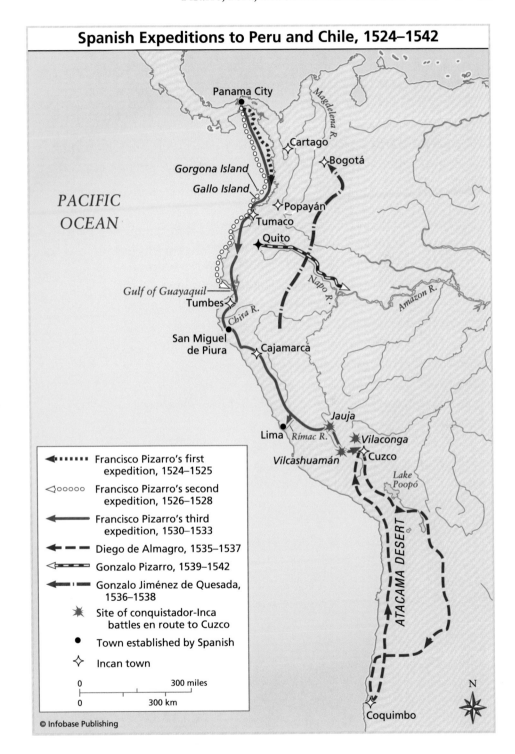

Spanish Expeditions to Peru and Chile, 1524–1542

Panama City

Cartago

Magdalena R.

Bogotá

Gorgona Island

Gallo Island

Popayán

**PACIFIC
OCEAN**

Tumaco

Quito

Gulf of Guayaquil

Tumbes

Chira R.

Napo R.

Amazon R.

San Miguel
de Piura

Cajamarca

Jauja

Lima   *Rímac R.*

Vilaconga

Vilcashuamán

Cuzco

*Lake
Poopó*

◀······ Francisco Pizarro's first
expedition, 1524–1525

◁ooooo Francisco Pizarro's second
expedition, 1526–1528

◀———— Francisco Pizarro's third
expedition, 1530–1533

◀– – – Diego de Almagro, 1535–1537

◁■━■━ Gonzalo Pizarro, 1539–1542

◀–·– Gonzalo Jiménez de Quesada,
1536–1538

✳ Site of conquistador-Inca
battles en route to Cuzco

● Town established by Spanish

✧ Incan town

ATACAMA DESERT

N

0   300 miles

0   300 km

Coquimbo

© Infobase Publishing

and traveled 150 miles (241 km) upriver. The ships quickly became lost in the maze of the Amazon delta. Most of the expedition—including Orellana—died from starvation, disease, or Native American attacks. Orellana's grave was never found. Only his wife and a few survivors lived to tell the tale.

SPAIN'S LEGACY

By 1600, Spain controlled much of the western half of South America. Armed resistance by Native Peoples continued for centuries, but the face of South America was changed forever by foreign intervention. Only the most remote parts of the continent were untouched by the conquest. Some of these lands remain unexplored to this day.

5

Cabeza de Vaca's Epic Journey

CABEZA DE VACA WAS TREASURER OF PÁNFILO NARVÁEZ'S expedition. They were authorized by King Charles V to conquer and govern lands "from the Rio de las Palmas to the Island of Florida." This region stretched from northeastern Mexico to Florida, across the present-day states of Texas, Louisiana, Mississippi, and Alabama.

The expedition, which left Spain on June 17, 1527, was nearly destroyed before it started. Storms battered Narváez's ships on three occasions before they successfully reached the coast of Florida on April 12, 1528. Desperate from loss of food, troops, and horses, the Spaniards searched for provisions after landing near Tampa Bay. They soon captured four Timucua Indians. The Timucua village possessed not only supplies of maize but small amounts of gold. The Timucua were eager for the Spaniards to leave and told them that there was much gold in the province of Apalache in northwestern Florida.

Narváez ordered his ships to sail parallel to the coast. De Vaca warned of the danger of heading into strange territory with few supplies, no interpreter, and no permanent base to which they could return if they lost contact with one another.

Narváez reached Apalache (present-day Tallahassee) seven weeks later. His men were starving and sore from carrying equipment over miles of rough trails. The people of the Apalache were suspicious of the Spanish. That suspicion turned to fury when the intruders took one of their chiefs hostage. The Apalache left the Spanish in possession of a town, but attacked them repeatedly. Narváez abandoned his mission and marched toward the coast in hope of finding his ships.

ESCAPE BY SEA

When Narváez reached the sea near today's Panama City, Florida, he realized that separating from his fleet had been a big mistake. The starving Spaniards stayed alive by butchering their horses and raiding Native American villages. The Native Peoples fought back. "With death as our only prospect," Cabeza de Vaca recalled, the Spaniards decided to flee by sea. The conquistadores' lack of experience in boat building showed in their escape barges. When 250 men crowded aboard the five vessels on September 22, 1528, the sides of the dangerous crafts floated only six inches above the water.

The survivors drifted westward along the coast for a month. Many died of thirst or from drinking seawater. By November 6, only de Vaca's barge remained. The rest of the expedition, including Narváez, had died or disappeared. The survivors landed on a sandy isle off the coast of Texas, probably Galveston Island. The starving men were fed by Karankawa Indians and again set sail. The barge overturned within sight of land, drowning several of the Spaniards. The freezing survivors were saved but treated like slaves by the Karankawa.

Only 15 of the 80 Spaniards survived the harsh winter. Cabeza de Vaca observed the dress, languages, bodily processes, work habits, funeral rites, and wedding customs of the Karankawa. He also acted as a medicine man. Protesting that they had no real powers, he and his companions agreed to the demands of the Karankawa that they heal the sick. "The way we treated them was to make over them the sign of the cross while breathing on them, recite a Pater Noster and Ave Maria, and pray to God, Our Lord, as best we could to give them good health and inspire them to do us some favors." To the Spaniards' surprise, their patients declared themselves healed.

When it was time for the Karankawa to leave their seasonal lodges on the coast, they took their Spanish prisoners except de Vaca. He was too ill to travel. After a year of abuse by the Karankawa who remained behind, he fled to live inland with the Charruco, who treated him better. He became a trader, which allowed him to travel freely for four years among the warring tribes of east Texas. He learned that the scattered

After surviving Pánfilo de Narváez's failed expedition, Cabeza de Vaca and three other survivors traveled by foot across present-day Texas and through Mexico. They met and lived with indigenous peoples, sometimes as captives. Cabeza de Vaca's experiences changed him into a sympathetic advocate for the indigenous peoples.

survivors of the Narváez expedition were either near death or had been killed by inland tribes.

De Vaca's freedom ended when he was enslaved by the Guevenes tribe. They mistreated him and constantly threatened to kill him. During this period of captivity, however, he was reunited with three survivors of the expedition: Alonso del Castillo Maldonado, Andrés Dorantes de Carranza, and Dorantes's North African slave, Estéban. Eventually, they escaped their captors and began to walk west. De Vaca and his companions depended on many Native American tribes for guidance. No maps were used, but descriptions of rivers, mountains, and other terrain they crossed provided enough clues to fuel several interpretations. Early scholars place the route across Texas along the Colorado or Pecos rivers, descending southwest to El Paso before continuing west. Later theories propose that they walked south across the Río Grande, through the present Mexican border states of Nuevo León, Coahuila, and Chihuahua. They then recrossed the Río Grande and followed the river northwest toward the El Paso area. The group next traveled southwest across northern Chihuahua, crossed the Sierra Madre Occidental mountain range, and reached the upper Río Yaqui. There they felt for the first time that they might actually reach home.

In April 1536, de Vaca, Estéban, and some Native Americans went in search of Spaniards who they thought were nearby. After several days, they found a Spanish slaving party. "I overtook four of them on horseback, who were astonished at the sight of me, so strangely dressed as I was, and in the company of Indians," Cabeza de Vaca recalled. "They stood staring at me for a time, so confounded that they neither hailed me nor drew near me to make an inquiry." The Spanish slaving party was fed by the "medicine men" and the 600 Native Americans traveling with them. Still de Vaca had to argue with the slavers to prevent them from kidnapping the Native Americans. The slavers eventually agreed to guide Castillo, Dorantes, Estéban, and de Vaca into Spanish-held Mexico. On July 25, 1536, the men arrived in Mexico City more than eight years after landing in Florida.

CABEZA DE VACA IN SOUTH AMERICA

De Vaca's experiences among the indigenous peoples had transformed him into a forceful advocate on their behalf. Although he wanted Spain

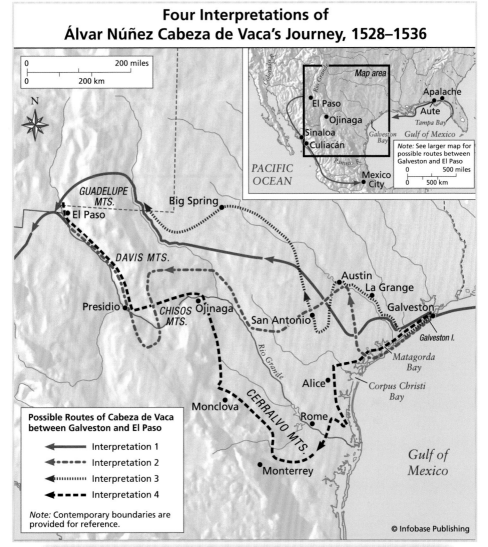

Four Interpretations of Álvar Núñez Cabeza de Vaca's Journey, 1528–1536

Since no maps were used during their travels, it is impossible to know the exact route taken by Cabeza de Vaca and his companions. This map shows four possible routes of Cabeza de Vaca's journey.

and the Christian religion to expand their control in the New World, he believed that such control could only happen by treating Native Americans with kindness. Charles V appointed de Vaca *adelantado* [administrator] of La Plata, which included all of present-day Paraguay, Argentina, Uruguay, and much of southern Brazil, Chile, and Bolivia.

He had the right to conquer, settle, profit from, and govern this vast territory. De Vaca attempted the trip overland through unexplored mountainous jungles. He and his men became the first Europeans to see Iguaçu Falls, which today mark the border between Argentina, Brazil, and Paraguay.

When he finally arrived at Asunción on March 11, 1542, de Vaca instituted new laws to protect the rights of the Native Peoples. He left Asunción on an exploratory mission for western Paraguay in September 1543. His attempts to find an overland route to Peru resulted only in the expedition being worn by starvation, Native American attacks, and disease. When de Vaca returned to Asunción after a six-month absence, he was arrested by resentful colonists and shipped to Spain in chains. He was tried on a number of false charges and sentenced to banishment in North Africa. Charles V lightened the sentence, but the damage to de Vaca's career was already done. He died around 1557 in Spain, poor and forgotten.

The story of the Narváez expedition survivors had an enormous effect upon exploration. It encouraged other expeditions and provided Europeans with the first realistic measurements of North America. It also provided valuable accounts of flora and fauna and detailed descriptions of Native societies living between the Gulf of Mexico and Spanish-held Mexico.

6

Hernando de Soto and "La Florida"

HERNANDO DE SOTO AND HIS MEN WERE THE FIRST EUROPEANS to see the Mississippi River. However, his journey was one of the most dramatic failures of Spanish exploration. He failed to find riches and used violence against Native Americans that shocked even some contemporary Spaniards. Yet his expedition contributed to Europeans' knowledge of the New World.

De Soto was leader of Francisco Pizarro's cavalry. He returned to Spain a wealthy man in 1536, but he soon grew restless. He asked Charles V for permission to return to the New World. The king appointed him governor of Cuba and granted him permission to explore and conquer "La Florida." These lands included the Florida peninsula and the area from the Carolinas to Texas.

Every explorer who preceded de Soto into La Florida had met with disaster. Yet de Soto was not easily intimidated. He interested a group of Spanish noblemen in his plan. The idea also attracted Portuguese volunteers. One wrote about the journey under the pen name "A Fidalgo [Gentleman] of Elvas." His memoirs, along with those of Rodrigo Ranjel and Luis Hernández de Biedma are the only first-person descriptions of the expedition's bloody progress.

LANDING IN LA FLORIDA

De Soto spent a year in Cuba planning for his Florida venture. He hired soldiers and armed them with crossbows and primitive guns called harquebuses. They had Irish wolfhounds trained as ferocious "war dogs."

He also gathered the craftsmen needed to run a colony, such as shoe-makers and tailors. He purchased food and trade items and packed hundreds of shackles and iron collars for slaves. When all preparations were complete, the force included some 620 men and 223 horses.

On May 1, 1539, de Soto's ships approached Florida's west coast. They sailed into a bay he named Espíritu Santu (Holy Spirit). As supplies were slowly unloaded, eager conquistadores rode into the surrounding marshland. They chased a group of Native Americans. They were shocked when one of the fleeing men pleaded for his life in Spanish.

The man was Juan Ortiz. He had been sent by Narváez's wife a decade earlier to find her husband. When Ortiz and his party landed in Florida in 1528, he and another Spaniard had been captured by Native Americans. Ortiz's companion was killed immediately. The tribe began to roast Ortiz alive over a coal fire. The chief's daughter convinced her father to spare the young Spaniard's life. Soon after, she saved Ortiz's life a second time. She warned him to flee before he was to be killed as a sacrifice. Ortiz escaped to the protection of a nearby tribe. He was living with them when news arrived that ships were sailing along the coast.

De Soto was thrilled to find Ortiz. He now had a translator. De Soto began to send military scouts inland. They did not find treasure. Instead, they were bogged down in swamps. There they were easy targets for hostile Native Americans. The furious de Soto suspected one Native American guide of leading the Europeans in circles. The guide was thrown to the dogs, which tore him to pieces.

By mid-July, the Europeans were starving in the humid, insect-ridden Florida summer. Instead of gold, they found only poor villages. Often, the local people burned their homes and fled with food stores before the Europeans arrived. De Soto left 100 men on the coast and sent most of the ships back to Cuba for more supplies. He ordered the rest of his party to march inland. There was no turning back.

De Soto's hungry army struggled northward. Native Peoples along the way who refused to supply food or information were tortured, raped, or killed. Others were chained and used as slaves to carry the Europeans' equipment. Starving soldiers often ate maize (corn) raw. They also ate chestnuts and whatever else they found.

Some Native tribes welcomed Hernando de Soto and his expedition, while others feared their approach. De Soto and his men were particularly brutal toward the indigenous peoples, killing, torturing, and enslaving them for food or information.

De Soto began taking hostages to prevent attacks on the indigenous peoples. On September 15, the expedition arrived at the Native American town of Napituca, in northern Florida. Seven Timucua chiefs asked to meet de Soto. Friendly Paracoxi Indians, however, told Ortiz that the Timucua were planning an ambush. De Soto rode onto the field as agreed. At his signal, a trumpet sounded and his cavalry charged. It took all night for the conquistadores to defeat the Timucua fighters. They tied the survivors to posts and used them as live archery targets.

De Soto's men headed northwest. Near modern-day Tallahassee, de Soto camped for the winter. That winter, a young indigenous captive named Perico told the Europeans that he knew of gold mines to the north. The land, he claimed, was called Cofitachequi and was ruled by a woman. In March 1540, Perico guided de Soto into present-day southern Georgia. There the Native Americans were friendlier. They offered the Europeans food, porters, and guides. In return, de Soto built large wooden crosses in the center of several towns and lectured the townspeople on the blessings of Christianity.

THE *REQUERIMIENTO*

Mistreatment of the indigenous peoples was against the declared wishes of Spanish royalty, who felt themselves morally obliged to bring Christianity to the Americas. To protect the Native Americans, while continuing to explore and colonize, King Ferdinand directed a council of theologians to define when military action might be taken against the indigenous peoples. The result was a long legal document called the *requerimiento*, which means "requirement." Conquistadores like de Soto were required to read the document aloud whenever they moved into lands inhabited by Native Americans.

The requerimiento demanded that the Native Americans "acknowledge the Church as the ruler and superior of the whole world" under the authority of the pope and the rulers of Spain. It demanded that Native Americans consent to religious instruction by priests. Refusal was equal to a declaration of war.

Conquistadores often read the complex document too quietly for the audience to hear. In most cases, the indigenous peoples simply could not understand the Spanish. Yet, throughout the exploration of the Americas, conquistadores used the requerimiento as justification for conquest of any land where their entry was opposed.

Within six weeks, however, the Europeans' supplies were again gone. Starving Native American slaves were released and told to fend for themselves, far inside South Carolina. Perico finally admitted that he was lost. He escaped being thrown to the dogs, for he was the only Native American whose language the translator Ortiz understood. On April 26, four Native Americans were captured near a deserted village. After de Soto ordered one of them burned to death, the others revealed that Cofitachequi was only two days away.

The female chieftain of Cofitachequi welcomed de Soto warmly near the present site of Camden, South Carolina. "She crossed in the canoes and spoke to the Governor quite gracefully and at her ease," Ranjel remembered. "She was a young girl of fine bearing; and she took off a string of pearls which she wore on her neck, and put it on the Governor as a necklace to show her favor and to gain his will." The Europeans spent a week enjoying the hospitality of the people of Cofitachequi.

Cofitachequi was the first place the expedition visited that promised any treasure. De Soto and his men searched local tombs, where they found bodies decorated with pearls. The Europeans removed 200 pounds of pearls from the mausoleum. The chieftain was willing to give them even more. However, crimes committed by de Soto's soldiers soon turned the people of Cofitachequi against them. When de Soto announced to the chieftain that he was leaving to search for richer lands, she refused him food or porters. He responded by taking her hostage. She managed to escape days later.

THE BATTLE OF MABILA

For two months, de Soto's expedition wandered through North Carolina and Tennessee. They crossed the Appalachian Mountains and turned into Alabama. At Coça, near modern-day Childersburg, they rested for a month under the protection of a Creek chief, who was repaid for his kindness by being taken hostage. Then they continued to head southwest, down the Alabama River to the Tombigbee River. On October 10, they met Chief Tascalusa. He was the most imposing chief they had met yet. "His appearance was full of dignity," the Gentleman of Elvas wrote. "He was a tall person, muscular, lean, and symmetrical. He was the suzerain of many territories, and of a numerous people, being equally feared by his vassals and the neighboring nations."

Tascalusa offered de Soto peaceful passage through his lands. After being entertained by Tascalusa's men, however, de Soto refused to let him return home. De Soto demanded male slaves to use as porters and 100 women. Tascalusa gave de Soto 400 men. He said that he would provide the women when they reached the nearby town of Mabila.

De Soto approached Mabila, near the present site of Mobile, Alabama. He was told that its people were stockpiling weapons. They were also summoning warriors from the countryside. De Soto ignored the warnings and rode into Mabila on October 18, 1540. He and a dozen of his men were greeted with dancing and singing. The Spaniards noticed, however, that the houses around them were filled with armed men. When Tascalusa disappeared into a house and refused to come out, one of de Soto's officers grabbed a passing Tascalusa. This started a fight, and de Soto's men began dropping under a hail of arrows. The wounded Spaniards fought their way out of the town. De Soto regrouped his forces and torched Mabila. They killed between 2,500 and 3,000 townspeople. Many jumped into the flames or hanged themselves rather than be captured and enslaved.

The badly wounded expedition rested for a month at Mabila. De Soto learned that Spanish ships were at the coast, only six days away, but he kept this news a secret. If he left now, his expedition would be considered a failure. Even the Cofitachequi pearls had been destroyed in the Mabila blaze. Determined to return home as a success, de Soto turned his expedition inland.

The group passed a peaceful winter among the Chickasaw. When it was time to leave, de Soto demanded porters from the tribe. The night before his planned departure, the Chickasaw attacked. They would have massacred the entire camp if the Europeans' terrified horses had not stampeded and thrown the ambush into chaos.

On Saturday, May 21, 1541, de Soto's men reached the Mississippi River, which they called the Río Grande. They saw it as simply another obstacle to overcome. Four barges were built; on June 8, the expedition crossed to the west bank. The fruitless search for treasure dragged on into southwestern Arkansas. De Soto's men and their slaves spent the winter snaring rabbits. Almost half of the 620 men who had marched from Florida, including translator Juan Ortiz, were now dead. Most of their horses were lame. De Soto finally decided to turn toward the Gulf of Mexico.

Near what is now Ferriday, Louisiana, the expedition entered a Native American town called Guachoya. The Guachoyans seemed friendly. They told de Soto that the neighboring people of Nilco were preparing to attack the Europeans. De Soto, however, was suspicious. He sent his cavalry into Nilco, and they slaughtered all but a few of its people. The Guachoyans watched the massacre, then rushed to sack the victims' homes.

By now it was clear to de Soto and his men that their expedition had failed. No gold had been discovered. Many in the ranks now hated the constant warring with Native Americans, which had gained them nothing. De Soto was seriously ill with fever. Even if he safely led the survivors back to Cuba, his reputation would be ruined.

His fever worsened on May 21, 1542. He called his officers together, thanked them, confessed his sins, and named Luis de Moscoso as his successor. De Soto died the next day and was secretly buried. De Soto had told the Guachoyans that he was immortal; they, however, noticed his absence and a mound of fresh grave dirt. The Spaniards dug up their leader at night, weighted his corpse with stones, and dropped him in the middle of the Mississippi River. The Gentleman of Elvas heard Moscoso tell the suspicious Guachoyan chief that "the Governor was not dead, but only gone into the heavens" and would return soon.

MOSCOSO TAKES COMMAND

Moscoso asked the members of the expedition what direction they wanted to take next. Lacking shipbuilding tools, the majority agreed to leave the river and march toward Mexico. They still hoped to discover riches along the way. For the next four months, the expedition struggled through northern Louisiana into east Texas, constantly battling with Native tribes. In October, they were near the present site of Austin, Texas. They tortured Native Americans to get information and learned that only barren deserts lay ahead. Moscoso called the expedition's leaders together near the present site of Austin. Winter was approaching and supplies were low. Despite finding turquoise and cotton, Moscoso ordered the group to turn back toward the "great river," the Mississippi.

After a grueling march, Moscoso and his men eventually reached the river. They took over the town of Aminoya, whose inhabitants were

Because the Guachoyans believed he was a god, de Soto's men had to keep his death a secret. They secretly buried his body, but the Guachoyans noticed the dirt mound. In the middle of the night, the Spaniards dug up his body and sank it in the middle of the Mississippi River.

reduced to starvation when the Europeans seized their food supplies. By spring 1543, the Europeans had built seven ships from local wood and nails made by melting down slave chains. Moscoso ordered all but his closest allies to dismiss their slaves. Amid much weeping, 500 Native American men, women, and children were abandoned in hostile territory, far from their homes.

On July 2, 1543, 322 surviving Europeans and 100 slaves set forth onto the Mississippi River. The Europeans stole maize from houses along the river and burned the first town they found. The next day, Native Americans approached the Europeans in canoes, offering friendship. As soon as they were within range, however, they rained arrows on the Europeans. Two dozen Spanish soldiers took to canoes to attack their pursuers. The Native Americans simply capsized them. The armor-laden conquistadores sank to the river bottom.

The drifting survivors reached the mouth of the Mississippi River 17 days later. A vote was taken, and they decided to proceed westward along the coast rather than risk voyaging across the Gulf of Mexico in the rickety boats. Juan de Añasco briefly convinced the party to try a sea route to speed their progress. Drinking water quickly began to run out. Storms and mosquitoes tormented them as they followed the coastline westward. In September 1543, 52 days after leaving the Mississippi, the survivors reached the mouth of the Río Pánuco, near the future site of Tampico, Mexico. For four days they tried to sail upriver against the current. They gave up and walked the rest of the way to the nearest Spanish settlement. "In their clothing of deerskin," the Gentleman of Elvas wrote, "they all went directly to the church, to pray and return thanks for their miraculous preservation."

The appearance of 311 survivors was a shock to Spanish authorities. They had long assumed that the entire group was dead. Accounts of the survivors described La Florida as a rugged, dangerous land. It could not be colonized easily. It was also not a country, like Peru, where fabulous wealth made peril worth the risk. De Soto's experience had a chilling effect on exploration of Florida for a century.

7

Coronado and the Seven Cities

WITH THE WEALTH OF MEXICO AND PERU ALREADY GLITTERING in their minds, Spanish treasure hunters looked north in the late 1530s. They dreamed they might find a new Tenochtitlán or Cuzco in the unexplored lands of what would become the United States. One of the first and greatest journeys of discovery into the heart of North America was led by Francisco Vásquez de Coronado. Members of his *entrada*, or expedition, were the first Europeans to meet the pueblo-dwelling peoples of the American Southwest. They were the first to see the Grand Canyon. They were also the first to see the Great Plains, traveling alongside Native American tribes whose survival depended on buffalo herds so vast that they covered the landscape as far as the eye could see. For centuries, however, Coronado's amazing entrada was forgotten, seen simply as a business venture whose failure cost its investors their fortunes.

Coronado's expedition was one of the best-documented journeys of its time. It was described by Coronado himself in letters to Antonio de Mendoza, the viceroy of New Spain. Others who described it were soldiers. They included the anonymous author of a document known as the *Relación del Suceso* (Story of the Event), or Captain Juan Jaramillo, or Pedro de Casteñeda, who recorded his experiences 20 years after marching from Mexico to present-day Kansas and back.

The Spanish expedition northward was sponsored by Mendoza. Mendoza had heard rumors of great cities to the north from the survival accounts of Cabeza de Vaca and his companions. Mendoza also had competition. His political rival, Hernán Cortés was funding a sailing expedition from Mexico's Pacific coast. Hernando de Soto had received a royal grant to explore La Florida. Mendoza thought competitors might beat him to the allegedly fabulously wealthy Seven Cities of Cíbola. This region was supposedly found north of Mexico's frontier.

Mendoza decided to send a small expedition north before investing heavily in the project. On March 7, 1539, the group left Culiacan, near the west-central coast of Mexico. Its official leader was Franciscan friar Marcos de Niza, a veteran of expeditions in Peru and Central America. The real leader, however, was Estéban, the experienced survivor of the Narváez and Cabeza de Vaca expeditions. Estéban retraced the roads by which he had come south through the Sonora Valley. Two months later the expedition reached the present Sonora-Arizona border. Niza sent Estéban ahead with orders to report any significant discoveries. It was a logical strategy, for the region's inhabitants remembered

Above is the Pueblo of Acoma in New Mexico. It is one of the legendary gold-filled "Seven Cities of Cíbola." Several expeditions were organized to seek out these mythical cities of unlimited riches. It is now believed that the mica-inflected clay of the adobe pueblos may have created an optical illusion when inflamed by the setting sun.

and got along well with Estéban. He was more than 200 miles (321 km) ahead of the main party when he reached the outskirts of Cíbola.

Several tales relate what may have happened when Estéban arrived at the first of the "Seven Cities." One legend says that Estéban sent the leaders of Cíbola a ceremonial gourd, which he had used in the past as a peace sign. At Cíbola, however, red feathers attached to the gourd were interpreted as a threat of war, and Estéban was killed. Another story says that the elders of Cíbola were irritated by Estéban's demands for turquoise and women and killed him.

News of Estéban's violent death terrified Fray Niza, and he fled back to Mexico City. Despite his hasty retreat, Niza reported to Mendoza that he had seen Cíbola from a distance. Rodrigo de Albornoz, treasurer of New Spain, described in a letter what Niza claimed to have learned of the people of the Seven Cities:

SEVEN CITIES OF CÍBOLA

Spain's search for seven rich cities north of the Mexican frontier appears to have begun with the childhood memories of Tejo. He was an indigenous slave owned by Nuño Beltrán de Guzmán, the brutal first governor of New Spain. Tejo told Guzmán that when he was a boy, his father had "gone into the back country with fine feathers to trade for ornaments, and that when he came back, he brought large amounts of gold and silver, of which there was a large amount in that country. He went with him once or twice, and saw some very large villages which compared with Mexico [City] and its environs. He had seen seven large towns which had streets of silver workers."

Guzmán led an expedition in 1530 to search for these "Seven Cities," but the venture ended when his followers mutinied in the harsh terrain of northwestern Mexico. In 1536, however, when Cabeza de Vaca's party emerged from the desert and told Mendoza they had heard of powerful villages to the north, Mendoza and other speculators assumed the Narváez expedition survivors were speaking of the Seven Cities.

They have houses built of stone and lime, being of three stories, and with great quantity of turquoises set in doors and windows. Of animals there are camels and elephants and cattle of our kind as well as wild ones, hunted by the natives, and a great number of sheep like those of Peru, also other animals with a single horn reaching to their feet, for which reason they must feed sideways.

As they continued on their journey, the Spanish soon learned that such tales were more fiction than fact.

CORONADO STARTS NORTH

Mendoza believed Niza and told Francisco Vásquez de Coronado to lead a large expedition north. Coronado was governor of the northernmost province of New Spain, Nueva Galicia. He and most of the

The Seven Cities became known as Cíbola. The origin of the word *Cíbola* itself is uncertain. Some anthropologists claim this name was based on the name of a Zuni pueblo—Shivola. Another theory is that Cíbola was a Spanish mispronunciation of Ashiwi, the name by which the Zuni then called themselves. If so, it would have been logical for Estéban to report that Native American guides informed him that they had arrived at the communities of the Ashiwi—the cities of Cíbola. The Spanish later named the bison they were seeing cíbolo. They associated these animals with the same region as the legendary Seven Cities.

Part of the allure of the search for seven cities lay in religion. Explorers hoped that Cíbola might be the mythical Seven Cities of Antilia. According to legend, after the Muslim invasion of the Iberian Peninsula in A.D. 714, seven Spanish or Portuguese bishops crossed the Atlantic to the island of Antilia, some 2,500 miles (4,023 km) west of Europe. Here they founded a Christian utopia. While the fortune hunters in Coronado's expedition sought gold, priests hoped to connect the fabled wealth and religious harmony of the island of Antilia with the rest of the Christian world.

volunteers he enlisted were not experienced, battle-hardened conquistadores like Cortés and de Soto. Coronado was under strict orders from Mendoza to avoid mistreating any Native Americans he might encounter. The expedition grew to become an armed force of 336 Europeans, mostly Spaniards, and hundreds of Mexican "Indian allies." In addition, six Franciscan friars, 1,000 indigenous laborers, and more than 1,500 horses and pack animals joined the party. Fray Niza guided the group.

The expedition left Nueva Galicia on February 23, 1540. Coronado decided to travel ahead of his main army, joined by 75 men. By June they were at the present border of Mexico and Arizona. They ascended onto the Colorado Plateau, struggling over a rugged landscape. This was not the easy route and bountiful countryside promised by Fray Niza. The hungry, disheartened men were inexperienced in living off the land. Several died from eating poisonous "water hemlock" out of desperation.

Finally, on July 7, Coronado arrived at the Zuni pueblo of Háwi-kuh. This was the first settlement of Cíbola. The starving men were stunned. They found a dusty town of 200 stone dwellings. It was not the magnificent city described by Fray Niza. "When they got within sight of the first pueblo, which was Cíbola," Casteñeda recalled, "the curses that some hurled at Fray Marcos were such that God forbid they may befall him."

Zuni archers got ready to defend their homes. Coronado sent a message that he came in peace. As he later reported, "[T]hey, being a proud people, were little affected, because it seemed to them that we were few in number, and that they would not have any difficulty in conquering us." When Zuni arrows began to fly at the intruders, the Spaniards attacked and took Háwikuh by force. An uneasy peace eventually settled over the town, and Coronado asked the Zuni about the surrounding lands:

> I commanded them to have a cloth painted for me, with all the animals that they know in that country, and although they are poor painters, they quickly painted two for me, one of the animals and the other of the birds and fishes. . . . They tell me about seven cities which are at a considerable distance, which are like these, except that the houses there are not like these, but are made of earth, and small, and that they raise much cotton there.

This was unwelcome news. The expedition had hoped to find rich cities. Coronado sent Fray Niza back to Mexico City in disgrace. "I can assure you that he has not told the truth in a single thing that he said, but everything is the opposite of what he related, except the name of the cities and the large stone houses," Coronado wrote to Mendoza.

THE GRAND CANYON

In September 1540, Coronado ordered Pedro de Tovar, one of his captains, to search for the land of the Hopi Indians. Tovar rode 65 miles (104 km) into what is now northeastern Arizona. Inhabitants of the first Hopi settlement he reached had heard of the Spanish attack on Háwikuh and warned Tovar to stay away. While Tovar tried to negotiate with the Hopi, his impatient soldiers rushed forward, provoking a brief fight. After this the Spanish and Hopi traded information peacefully. Tovar returned to Coronado with news that a great river lay to the west.

Coronado immediately sent a second party, led by García López de Cárdenas, to investigate. In September 1540, 20 days away from the Hopi villages and the Painted Desert (in modern-day Arizona), Cárdenas and his men became the first Europeans to see the Grand Canyon. Casteñeda wrote:

> [They] came to the banks of a river, which seemed to be more than three or four leagues in an air line across to the other bank of the stream which flowed between them. The country was elevated and full of low, twisted pines, very cold, and lying open to the north. . . . They spent three days on this bank looking for a passage down to the river, which looked from above as if the water was 6 feet [1.8 m] across, although the Indians said it was half a league [about 1.5 miles] wide.

Cárdenas's party is thought to have reached the canyon's south rim near Moran Point. After the three "lightest and most agile men" in the group tried but failed to reach the river, Cárdenas and his men soon went on their way. They were more interested in finding drinking water than in exploring the giant canyon. Some 135 years passed before another European, Francisco Tomás Garcés, explored the Grand Canyon.

When he and a party were sent to scout out the Hopi, García López de Cárdenas became the first European to see the Grand Canyon, located in present-day northwestern Arizona. Pictured is the Grand Canyon, viewed from the south rim.

"ALARCÓN CAME THIS FAR"

Fray Niza had created the false impression that Cíbola was close enough to the Pacific coast to be supplied by sea. On May 9, 1540, Mendoza dispatched exploratory ships north into the Gulf of California. The supply-laden ships commanded by Hernando de Alarcón reached the mouth of the Colorado River, whose waters were colored red by silt. Alarcón tried sailing upriver. He met Yuma (Quechan) Indians who had heard of Estéban's death and Coronado's expedition. When the Yuma told Alarcón that Coronado was hundreds of miles inland, he abandoned his mission.

Meanwhile, Coronado surmised correctly that a reddish river he had crossed—the Little Colorado—eventually drained into the sea. In fact, the Little Colorado joins the main Colorado River in the Grand Canyon. He ordered Melchior Díaz to find Alarcón's supply ships, whose supply mission was part of the original plan. Díaz backtracked hundreds of miles south before taking an unknown route west to the Colorado. About 40 miles (64 km) from the gulf, Díaz found a tree scratched with writing. It read, "Alarcón came this far; there are letters at the foot of this tree." Díaz explored the area for six days before crossing the Colorado. He rode south into the deserts of southeastern California. He died after falling from his horse onto his own spear. As was the case with the Cárdenas discovery, no explorers would visit the area for another century.

THE CAPTIVE OF CICUYÉ

On August 29, while Cárdenas was marching northwest toward the Grand Canyon, Coronado sent Hernando de Alvarado and 20 men eastward. They traveled across what is now central New Mexico. Alvarado's guide was a chieftain the Spaniards nicknamed Bigotes, or "Whiskers," because of his long mustaches. Bigotes came from a pueblo 250 miles (402 km) east of Háwikuh. It was called Cicuyé.

Four days into their journey, Alvarado's men became the first Europeans to see the Acoma Pueblo, a Keres Indian town built on top of a flat-topped land formation called a mesa (Spanish for "table"). Acoma had existed for at least 500, possibly 1,000, years before the arrival of the Spaniards. The town still exists today. It is one of the oldest continuously inhabited communities in North America.

Alvarado continued his journey. He reached the Río Grande near the present site of Albuquerque, New Mexico, deep in the Native American region then known as Tiguex. He sent word to Coronado that he had found a suitable place for the expedition to spend the winter. After exploring northward along the Río Grande as far as Taos Pueblo, Alvarado continued east to Cicuyé, which was known to other pueblos as Pecos. The enormous pueblo was a significant trading center connecting the Pueblo Indians of the southwest with the hunting tribes of the Great Plains. The people of Cicuyé had never been defeated in battle and were feared by other tribes. They felt no reason to be intimidated by the Spanish and welcomed them warmly.

While awaiting Coronado's arrival in Tiguex, Alvarado asked his hosts about lands to the east. The Pecos introduced him to one of their captives, a Pawnee or Wichita from Kansas or Nebraska. The Spaniards nicknamed him El Turco, "the Turk," because something about his head-gear reminded them of the Turkish. When Coronado arrived at Tiguex, Alvarado presented him with El Turco. The captive convinced the Spaniards that his home, Quivira, was a place of fabulous wealth and natural wonders. El Turco told Coronado that fish in Quivira were as large as horses and swam in rivers 5 miles (8 km) wide: "He stated further that the lord of that land took his siesta under a large tree from which hung numerous golden bells, and he was pleased as they played in the wind. He added that the common table service of all was generally of wrought silver, and that the pitchers, dishes, and bowls were made of gold."

El Turco had no proof of his fantastic claims but insisted that at the time of his capture he had worn gold bracelets, which Bigotes had taken. Alvarado seized Bigotes and another chieftain, then brought them to Coronado. They tortured the men to produce the golden bracelets. No confession resulted, and the people of Cicuyé were furious. Still, Coronado was certain that El Turco was telling the truth.

A BLOODY WINTER

The Pecos of Cicuyé soon grew tired of Coronado and his men. When winter began, the Spanish and their Mexican Indian allies were completely unprepared. Their solution was to force local people from their homes. Spanish thefts of food, clothing, blankets, and firewood from surrounding pueblos increased as the winter grew colder. Tension increased when Coronado refused to punish a Spaniard accused of raping a Pecos woman. To retaliate, the Pecos murdered one of a Coronado's men and killed a large number of their horses. Within days, the Spaniards and the Pecos were fighting a war.

Spanish soldiers destroyed the pueblo of Arenal and captured 70 of its defenders. The soldiers offered them a chance to surrender, but Coronado was angry and had given no orders to negotiate. He ordered 50 captives to be burned at the stake and slaughtered the rest when they resisted. By the time the war ended in March 1541, tribes throughout the region knew Coronado's words of friendship could not be trusted.

KINGDOM OF QUIVIRA

Relations with Native Americans were more peaceful during the rest of Coronado's expedition. In April 1541, he took a small force eastward to find the kingdom of Quivira. El Turco led the expedition across the plains of northwestern Texas, later called the Llano Estacado (Staked Plains). The land was so featureless that they made piles of buffalo bones and dung to mark their path. One rider who wandered away disappeared forever in the endlessly flat landscape.

Coronado's men were the first Europeans to meet a Native American tribe of the Great Plains. They called this western Apache group Querechos. These nomadic people hunted bison and traveled across the plains on foot, trading hides with more permanently settled tribes. Horses were still unknown to the Plains Indians. They transported their belongings on wooden pole frames that were tied to dogs. They treated the Spanish with great hospitality.

As Coronado crossed the north Texas and Oklahoma panhandles into present-day Kansas, he began to lose faith in El Turco's guidance. Another indigenous captive, Isopete, accused El Turco of lying. Low on supplies, Coronado continued onward with only 30 horsemen. The rest turned back to Tiguex. They were now led by Isopete, who offered to guide the company in exchange for his freedom. On June 29, 1541, they reached a Wichita village by the Arkansas River near the present-day town of Ford, Kansas. This, Isopete explained, was Quivira, home of a tribe the Europeans later called the Wichita. The Spaniards realized that, like Fray Niza, El Turco had lied. Coronado continued to explore the region for more than a month, finally stopping near the present site of Salina, Kansas.

The land was rich with game, clean water, and fruit trees. But there was no gold. When El Turco secretly appealed to the Quivirans to kill the Spaniards, his captors strangled him. A few days later, Coronado freed Isopete, planted a cross to "take possession" of the land for Spain, and returned west, hoping to rejoin his army before winter. Ironically, the expedition had come within only a few hundred miles of Hernando de Soto's floundering *entrada*, members of which were scouting along the lower reach of the Arkansas River after having recently discovered the Mississippi River.

Coronado's men found their way back across 1,000 miles (1,609 km) of grassy plains to their headquarters at Tiguex, arriving in October 1541. That winter, some members of the expedition discussed staying in Tierra Nueva, the "New Land," which would one day become

The Wichita, one of whose villages is depicted above, were one of many tribes Coronado met while exploring what is now the United States. Their villages of dome-shaped and grass-covered huts went as far south as San Antonio, Texas, and as far north as Great Bend, Kansas.

New Mexico. Some wanted to settle in Quivira, while others wanted to push even further eastward. They were still convinced there might be some truth to El Turco's tales of riches. In December, however, Coronado was gravely injured in a riding accident. While recovering, he declared that the expedition was over and ordered a return to Mexico.

Coronado arrived in Mexico in late 1542 after an absence of two and a half years. He left only a handful of settlers and missionaries in Tierra Nueva. He also left behind bitter memories of his cruelty, leaving a dangerous legacy for future explorers. Coronado died in Mexico City in 1554.

Coronado's expedition had surprisingly little impact on contemporary exploration. The public heard and cared little about its discoveries. It was seen merely as a failed commercial venture. When fresh rumors of great civilizations in the region reached south to Mexico in the 1580s, the expedition had been forgotten so completely that an entirely new wave of fortune seekers rushed to the Spanish court, pleading for permission to "discover" the same lands Coronado and his men had journeyed across.

Old soldiers like Casteñeda, Jaramillo, and the author of the *Relación del Suceso* recorded their memories, however, they lay undisturbed in Spanish archives for centuries. The expedition was dismissed and forgotten in Coronado's lifetime, but history later revealed it to be one of the great epics of exploring the Americas.

8

Exploring California

THE VOYAGES SPONSORED BY HERNÁN CORTÉS FAILED TO REVEAL much of California's coastline; the Spanish, however, stayed curious about what lay to the north. One of the endeavor's most enthusiastic sponsors was Cortés's political rival, Antonio de Mendoza, viceroy of New Spain. Mendoza chose Juan Rodríguez Cabrillo to lead an expedition north. Cabrillo was a Spanish shipbuilder and soldier who had fought in the conquests of Cuba, Mexico, and Central America.

On June 27, 1542, Cabrillo's fleet set sail from the tiny Mexican port of Navidad, near Manzanillo on Mexico's west-central coast. Cabrillo sailed up the western coast of Baja, California. Three months after leaving Mexico, he sailed into a harbor that he described in his log as "sheltered and very good." Cabrillo stepped ashore and claimed the land for Spain. He called the area San Miguel in honor of the archangel Michael. It would later be called San Diego.

THE BAY OF SMOKES

At San Diego, Cabrillo's men were met by the Ipai tribe. The Ipai had heard of Coronado's inland expedition. Cabrillo's log noted that the Ipai "made signs that they [Coronado's men] were killing many native Indians, and for this reason they were afraid." Cabrillo heard such stories repeatedly as he moved up the coast.

Cabrillo set off for nearby islands that were visible in the distance. He named them San Salvador and Victoria, after his ships. (Today the islands are known as Santa Catalina and San Clemente.) When Cabrillo returned to the mainland just south of present-day Los Angeles, the air was thick with smoke. The Native Americans were setting fires to improve the land for autumn crops. The fires also thinned the landscape for hunting game. The smoke was so thick that Cabrillo named the harbor Bahía de los Fumos, or "Bay of Smokes." Today it is San Pedro Bay.

Cabrillo found that tribes of friendly Native Americans lived along the coast. They were happy to trade food for glass beads and other items with which the Spanish had stocked their ships. When a storm drove Cabrillo back to a village named Ciucut, where he had earlier anchored near present-day Santa Barbara, he described the village and its ruler:

> The ruler of these pueblos is an old Indian woman, who came to the ships and slept for two nights on the captain's ship, as did many Indians. The pueblo of Ciucut appeared to be the capital of the rest, for they came there from other pueblos at the call of this ruler.

After several days of music and dancing, the Spaniards replenished their supplies and resumed the voyage north. A storm separated Cabrillo's flagship, the *San Salvador*, from the rest of the fleet off the rocky coast of Monterey. The *San Salvador* sailed alone up the coast as far as the Russian River (opposite present-day Santa Rosa) before turning back. He found the other ships near Monterey Bay. By then, winter had begun, making the frigid seas too dangerous for travel. Cabrillo ordered a retreat south to the calmer harbors at San Salvador (Santa Catalina) and other islands off the Bay of Smokes.

The local indigenous peoples were no longer welcoming. They were angered by constant Spanish demands for food and shelter. Around Christmas in 1542, Cabrillo rushed to help his men during a Native American attack. He jumped out of a boat and broke either his leg or his arm, and the wound became infected. Cabrillo died on January 3, 1543, after passing command to his pilot, Bartolomé Ferrer.

Ferrer resumed the voyage north in January 1543. The little fleet succeeded in passing the most northerly point it had reached earlier and struggled as far as 42° north latitude. This is just above the modern boundary between California and Oregon. The wooden fleet was no match for the wintry seas, which separated the ships and threatened to send them to the ocean bottom. Cold, hungry, and ill, the survivors found their way back to Navidad, Mexico, arriving on April 14, 1543.

The expedition had explored about 1,500 miles (2,414 km) of California coastline. The Spanish trading ships that began to sail between Mexico and the Philippines about this time would now have a better idea of what lay north of Baja California. Still, Spanish authorities considered the Cabrillo-Ferrer expedition to be of little importance. For Mendoza, the voyage was simply another expensive failure to find riches or routes to Asia or the Atlantic Ocean. The ships' logs were ignored and reports gathered dust and disappeared in Spanish archives. Cabrillo's and Ferrer's efforts were forgotten for nearly 60 years.

DRAKE IN CALIFORNIA

In the late 1500s, hostility between Catholic Spain and Protestant England turned the waters and ports of the Caribbean into a violent battle zone. Spanish treasure ships from the Caribbean were targets of English pirates, such as Sir Francis Drake. Spain's ports on the Pacific coasts, however, were safe. Spanish ships brought luxury goods, such as silk and porcelain, from Asia to Mexico. Silver shipments sailed from Peru to Panama. The goods were carried overland to Atlantic ports to be taken to Spain.

Drake was given unofficial permission by Queen Elizabeth I to attack and rob Spanish ships. If Drake was captured, however, the queen would deny any knowledge of his activities. His plan was to round South America and sail into the Pacific Ocean. Since English ships were never seen there, Spanish treasure ships and their ports could be caught unprepared and easily captured.

Drake's small fleet navigated through the dangerous Strait of Magellan, at the southern tip of South America. Soon after the ships emerged from the strait into the Pacific, they were seized by a violent storm that blew them southward. By the time the storm ended seven weeks later, Drake had been carried into open seas south of Tierra del Fuego. This was the group of islands south of the Strait of Magellan. He had discovered that the land there was a series of islands, not part of a continental mass. In his honor, the waters between South America and Antarctica were later named the Drake Passage.

In 1579, Francis Drake just missed San Francisco Bay when sailing along the western coast of North America. Because his charts, writings, and logs were destroyed, the exact place where he landed is in dispute. Some suggest Marin County, California, just north of San Francisco, while others claim it was Whale Cove, Oregon.

By the time Drake began plundering Spanish gold in the Pacific, shipwrecks, mutiny, and confusion had reduced his small fleet to his own flagship, the *Golden Hind*. Still, Drake's plan was a great success. He caught the Spanish off guard and the *Golden Hind* was soon packed with Spanish treasure. Drake now faced the problem of getting home to England. Instead of sailing again through the treacherous Strait of Magellan, he decided to sail north. He hoped to find the fictitious Northwest Passage, a sea route across the top of North America that would take him from the Pacific to the Atlantic Ocean. He probably sailed to the present-day border between the United States and Canada. There, the cold winter weather convinced him that a northerly passage to England was impossible.

Drake sailed south, searching for a harbor where he could repair his ship. In June 1579, the *Golden Hind* anchored near the future site of

San Francisco. When Drake landed, he was met by local Native Americans, thought to be the Coast Miwok. The Miwok were the original inhabitants of Marin County. Friendly toward the strangers, they guided the English to their village and placed a crown on Drake's head. Modern researchers suggest that the Miwok considered the strangers to be living representatives of dead ancestors.

Drake and his men explored some of the wooded countryside near the harbor. Their main concern was working to make the *Golden Hind* seaworthy. Before his departure, Drake named the northwest coast "Nova [New] Albion" and claimed it for Queen Elizabeth. On June 23, he sailed away from California. His voyage would take him around the globe, and he arrived in England in September 1580. Had his claim of land been pursued, California, not Virginia, might have become England's first colony in the New World.

VIZCAÍNO TRIES AGAIN

The task of learning about California's coast next fell to a merchant and would-be Spanish colonizer named Sebastián Vizcaíno. Vizcaíno set sail with three ships carrying 130 men on May 5, 1602. He was sponsored by New Spain's viceroy Gaspar de Zuñiga y Acevedo. Vizcaíno's patron ordered him to name every port he discovered after a Christian saint and claim it for Spain. He also was ordered not to rename any sites previously named by Cabrillo, Ferrer, or others.

Vizcaíno had little or no information from the earlier expeditions. As a result, he renamed lands discovered by earlier explorers as he slowly made his way up the California coast. San Salvador became Catalina and La Victoria became San Clemente, names by which both islands are still known. On the mainland, the harbor Cabrillo had christened San Miguel harbor was named after a Christian saint, San Diego de Acalá. Today it is simply known as San Diego. The coastline of modern California is dotted with other locations named by Vizcaíno: Santa Barbara, Point Conception, Carmel, and Año Nuevo.

In December 1602, Vizcaíno's ships sailed along the rocky, wooded shores of a bay he named Monterrey (now spelled Monterey) after his sponsor. He thought the area would be a good site for a permanent settlement:

There is fresh water in quantity and the harbor is very secure against all winds. The land is thickly peopled by Indians and is very fertile, in its climate and the quality of the soil resembling Castile, and any seed sown there will give fruit, and there are extensive lands fit for pasturage, and many kinds of animals and birds.

Vizcaíno's party was low on supplies. Many of the men were ill. One ship was sent back to Mexico, carrying the sick and news that a possible port had been found. The other two ships sailed north. Like Cabrillo, Vizcaíno failed to discover San Francisco Bay. The ships were barely seaworthy enough to continue and became separated in the turbulent ocean. Vizcaíno's sailors were in bad shape; many suffered from scurvy and the effects of eating rotten food. "The mouths of all were sore, and their gums were swollen larger than their teeth, so that they could hardly drink water," wrote Vizcaíno in his diary. "The ship seemed more like a hospital than a ship of an armada." Disease and cold took the lives of many of the sailors.

Vizcaíno's two ships never joined each other again during the rest of the expedition. Each struggled through the same overwhelming seas Ferrer had reached. They reached about 43° north, just north of the California-Oregon border. By the time orders were given to turn back, horrible conditions aboard the vessels had killed most of the crew members. Vizcaíno and the other survivors managed to reach Acapulco, Mexico, in March 1603, 10 months after they had embarked. He had fought—and noted—the contrary currents and winds, accurately charted the coastline, sounded the depths of bays, and explored the countryside whenever he landed. His main mission of finding a suitable harbor had been completed, but no attempt was made to settle Monterey until 1770.

Unlike so many Spanish explorers whose efforts ended in disgrace or death, Vizcaíno continued to enjoy a distinguished career as an explorer, international diplomat, military leader, and merchant. Thanks to the efforts of Cabrillo, Ferrer, and Vizcaíno, however, later explorers and missionaries were not venturing into the complete unknown when they reached coastal California.

FATHER KINO AND THE ISLAND OF CALIFORNIA

By the 1700s, Spain's strength as a world power was declining. The incredible wealth imported from the New World had been squandered in European wars, leaving Spain's economy in ruins. Large exploratory expeditions in search of new wealth were now a thing of the past. Colonists, many of whom were now American-born rather than immigrants, were organizing ranches, mines, and missions from Florida to New Mexico. Recent Pueblo Indian revolts in New Mexico left the frontier dangerous for explorers, unrewarding for newcomers hoping to make a living, and a challenge to Christian missionaries pursuing religious conversion of the region's native inhabitants.

Yet, European-born missionaries continued to arrive in the New World. Most were Franciscan and Jesuit priests. To them, the danger of entering hostile lands was an acceptable risk. Through their missionary activity, they found new routes between Mexico and California.

Father Eusebio Kino was an Italian-born Jesuit priest. When he arrived in Mexico in 1681, he knew a great deal about geography, cartography, and astrology. His first assignment was to set up a mission in Baja (Lower) California. He sailed from Mexico's Pacific coast across the Gulf of California with the 1683 colonizing expedition of Admiral Isidro Atondo y Antillón. The colony quickly failed, but a second attempt that year was a success. It resulted in exploration of the entire southern peninsula. When Kino returned to Mexico City in 1685, however, he was stranded there when a war between Spain and France left missionaries without funding.

Still devoted to the ideal of developing Baja California, Kino came up with a plan to establish mission communities near the northwestern coast of the Mexican mainland. The missions would support both themselves and further trips into California. Kino obtained approval for the project and set to work in 1687.

Kino's missionary territory turned out to be larger than he had planned. He was assigned to Pimería Alta (Upper Pimería), a district comprising present-day southwestern Arizona and northern Sonora State in Mexico. Pimería was named after its inhabitants, the Pima, an association of desert-dwelling tribes also known collectively by their Native American name, O'odham (The People).

San Xavier del Bac, near present-day Tucson, Arizona, was one of the many missions Eusebio Kino established in 1699. The original building was destroyed by the Apache in 1770. It was rebuilt with native labor from the Tohono O'odham nation between 1783 to 1797 and still serves this community.

Father Kino built his first mission along the San Miguel River in northern Sonora. He named it Nuestra Señora de los Dolores (Our Lady of Sorrows). The mission became the headquarters for his tireless exploring and missionary activities. During his lifetime, Kino established more than 20 missions, including San Xavier del Bac, near present-day Tucson, and Tumacácori (north of the modern border city of Nogales and now a U.S. National Historical Park). He introduced new crops, such as wheat, and domesticated animals, such as beef cattle and sheep. Mutual respect between the Pima and Father Kino helped the missions flourish.

Kino traveled many thousands of miles across unexplored lands on horseback. He made more than 40 journeys, ranging between 100 and 1,000 miles (160.9 and 1,609 km) each. He collected information and made the first accurate maps of the region and its rivers. Despite his success in Pimería, Kino never abandoned his hopes for Baja California.

Like many in Mexico, Kino believed that California was an island. In 1699, Yuma Indians near the western Gila River gave him blue abalone seashells like the ones he had seen years earlier on the Pacific coast of Baja California. He decided that if the shells could have been carried overland, perhaps it was possible to reach—and supply—California by land.

In the late 1690s, Kino journeyed to the northwest corner of Sonora where it borders California. He became convinced that the two regions were divided only by the Colorado River. At one point, he sighted land in the distance. He was sure it was California. On a later expedition, Kino and a small party of Pima rode south along the east bank of the Colorado, meeting tribes who ferried him over to the California shore in a basket. In 1702, he followed the Colorado all the way down to the Gulf of California. Kino added his findings to maps. For generations, however, the myth that California was an island was slow to disappear, even after Spanish missions lined the coastline of upper California.

EXPLORING UPPER CALIFORNIA

Father Kino died suddenly on March 15, 1711, in Magdalena, Sonora. In addition to the first accurate maps of Pimería Alta, the Gulf of California, and Baja California, he had proved that Baja California was a peninsula, not an island. Without the charismatic and industrious Kino to sustain the missions he founded, however, many of them declined.

An even stronger blow came in 1767 when Spain's King Charles III ordered all Jesuits expelled from Spain and its territories. He suspected them of promoting political unrest. Franciscan priests replaced the Jesuits. José de Gálvez was sent to Mexico to expel the Jesuits. Gálvez decided to strengthen Spain's hold on Alta (Upper) California. He wanted to protect Spanish claims against English and Russian challenges.

Gálvez journeyed to Baja California to organize an expedition. He put Captain Gaspar de Portolá in charge. Portolá would march his men up the California peninsula. Fray Junípero Serra, new president of the formerly Jesuit missions of Baja California, was to oversee the expedition's missionary aspect. Two ships, the *San Carlos* and the *San Antonio*, would sail up the coast and meet them near San Diego.

Land and sea expeditions all met as planned at San Diego on July 1, 1769. Scurvy had killed most of the sailors aboard the ships. Two days later, Serra described the area and its Ipai inhabitants in a letter to his friend and later biographer, Father Francisco Palou:

> *The tract through which we passed is generally very good land, with plenty of water. . . . We found vines of a large size, and in some cases quite loaded with grapes; we also found an abundance of roses, which appeared to be like those of Castile. We have seen Indians in immense numbers, and all those on this coast of the Pacific contrive to make a good subsistence on various seeds, and by fishing. The latter they carry on by means of rafts or canoes, made of tule [bullrush] with which they go a great way to sea. They are very civil. . . . We found on our journey, as well as in the place where we stopped, that they treated us with as much confidence and good-will as if they had known us all their lives. But when we offered them any of our victuals, they always refused them. All they cared for was cloth, and only for something of this sort would they exchange their fish or whatever else they had.*

Serra set to work building the first mission in the present state of California, at San Diego de Acala. Captain Portolá continued up the coast, following Gálvez's orders to reach the wonderful harbor Vizcaíno had reported in 1603 to exist at Monterey.

Portolá and his men arrived at Monterey on October 1, 1769. They did not recognize the bay because it did not fit Vizcaíno's grand description. They continued northward along the mountainous coast. One evening, a hunting party commanded by Sergeant José Francisco Ortega returned to camp. Fray Juan Crespi, the group's chaplain, noted in his diary, "[A]t about eight o'clock at night on the third [of November], the scouts came back from their exploration, firing off a salvo, and reported on arrival that they had come upon a great estuary, very broad, that must reach about eight or ten leagues inland." This strait—later named the Golden Gate—connected the Pacific Ocean with San Francisco Bay. Although Portolá did not yet realize it, Ortega and his scouts had discovered the perfect Pacific coast harbor, which previous explorers had repeatedly bypassed.

After a difficult journey during which they were forced to eat their mules to survive, Portolá and his men returned to San Diego on January 24, 1770. Fray Serra and others, however, were disappointed because Portolá had not found Monterey. Its discovery was more anticipated because of Vizcaíno's inflated description.

RETURN TO MONTEREY

A second attempt set out to find Monterey in mid-April. Serra sailed aboard the *San Antonio* and Portolá led a few dozen soldiers overland. The land expedition reached Monterey on May 24, 1770. When they discovered a large cross they had planted during their previous expedition, Portolá and his men realized they had found Monterey six months earlier but had just not recognized it. Lack of fresh water caused them to move their camp to nearby Carmel Bay.

When Serra joined the group, he celebrated Mass near the beach on June 3. Spanish soldiers "took possession" of the land in the name of King Charles III—228 years after Cabrillo's seaborne expedition had claimed the same coast for Spain.

The basic mission ordered by visitor-general Gálvez was accomplished. Colonization began in earnest, with smaller expeditions revealing California's valleys and the true dimensions of San Francisco Bay. Before his death in 1784, Serra traveled repeatedly along the California coastline. He founded nine missions: San Diego (1769), San Carlos Borromeo (1770), San Antonio (1771), San Gabriel (1771), San Luis Obispo

(1772), San Francisco (1776), San Juan Capistrano (1776), Santa Clara (1777), and San Buenaventura (1782). Twenty-one missions eventually lined Alta California's coast, from San Diego in the south to St. Francis Solano in the future town of Sonoma.

THE ROLE OF CALIFORNIA MISSIONS

The California mission system founded by Father Junípero Serra served both worldly and religious purposes. Militarily, missions reinforced Spain's claim to California against other European powers, particularly English mariners and Russian sea otter hunters descending the Pacific coastline. Each mission included a presidio, or fort, with a small number of soldiers.

Franciscan friars had more than one goal. Not only did they hope to convert Native Americans to Catholicism, but they also wanted to absorb local tribes into the Spanish empire. The indigenous peoples were required to live on mission grounds. They had to speak Spanish and wear European clothing. European crops were grown on mission farms. These included barley, beans, and wheat, replacing traditional indigenous foods such as berries, fruit, and nuts.

Deadly diseases and disruption to traditional life that accompanied European arrival in California took a severe toll in Native American lives. This was especially true in crowded mission living quarters. Harsh working conditions and anger over unpunished crimes against Native Americans by soldiers caused bloody revolts against the Franciscans. Native Americans protested when the Vatican considered elevating Father Serra to sainthood in the 1980s, while Serra's defenders replied by crediting him for introducing European culture to California.

Increasing numbers of colonists with neither military nor church duties began to arrive in California in the 1770s, but missions remained at the center of colonial life into the early 1800s. While their cultural role is controversial, the architecture of the missions remains one of the most historically important reflections of early Spanish America.

CAPTAIN ANZA AND FATHER GARCÉS

The new missions renewed interest in discovering a land route between Sonora and the Pacific coast. Supplying struggling California settlements by sea was dangerous and costly. An overland connection would help colonists to reach the coast in larger numbers. In 1773, permission to find a route was granted to Juan Bautista de Anza, a cavalry captain in command of the presidio of San Ignacio de Tubac, at the present-day southern Arizona town of Tubac.

Anza left Tubac on January 8, 1774, with 33 others, including Fray Francisco Garcés. Garcés, a Franciscan missionary, had already made trips from San Xavier del Bac along the Gila and Colorado rivers alone, much as Eusebio Kino had done decades earlier. Anza and Garcés both detailed the journey in official diaries.

They moved through the lands of the Yuma people. Starting on February 13, Anza became lost for 10 days in the sand dunes of southeastern California. "Seeing the generally disastrous condition of all of our riding animals and the impossibility of continuing the march with them," Anza wrote in his diary, he knew the expedition needed a new plan.

To get around the vast, shifting dunes, Anza's company went southwest into Baja California. They turned north to enter Alta California west of Mexicali. They struggled through hot deserts and winter snow in the San Jacinto Mountains. Anza arrived at San Gabriel Arcángel mission (east of the present city of Los Angeles) on March 22, 1774. There were not enough supplies for the entire expedition to continue, so Anza and four soldiers continued north with guides. They reached Monterey on May 1. The rest of the expedition returned to Yuma. Father Garcés set out on his own to look for a shortcut back to Sonora.

RETURN TO CALIFORNIA

Opening a supply route to California earned Anza a military promotion. His superiors asked him to organize a second expedition. They wanted to colonize the San Francisco Bay area. The expedition left on October 23, 1775. That night, a woman died from childbirth complications, but all of the other 240 colonists and 48 soldiers survived the 62-day trek. The survival rate was incredible, given the unpredictable supplies of water and food, violent winter weather, and bad roads. The colonists arrived at Monterey on March 10, 1776. In April, Anza departed Monterey for

Tubac. He left his lieutenant, José Joaquin Moraga, to lead the colonists the rest of the way to San Francisco.

Fray Garcés traveled with Anza's outbound 1775 colonizing group. He left the group at the future site of Yuma, Arizona. He founded a mission there. Then, Garcés set off alone on muleback. He followed the Colorado River upstream. He crossed the mountains of southern California and the Mojave Desert, and then found the Grand Canyon. He was the first European to see the canyonlands since Francisco Vásquez de Coronado's officer García López de Cárdenas visited them 135 years earlier.

FOUR CORNERS

Friars Francisco Atanasio Dominguez and Silvestre Velez de Escalante thought they could find an easier route to Monterey. Their plan was to travel inland north to Monterey's latitude and head west, thus avoiding the difficult terrain and hostile Native American tribes. On July 29, 1776, the two Franciscans set out from Santa Fe, New Mexico. Their group of 14 men included a cartographer, Captain Bernardo de Miera y Pacheco. They returned to Santa Fe on January 2, 1777, without ever seeing California, however, they had explored 1,800 miles (2,896 km) of the area known today as the Four Corners. In this region, the states of Arizona, New Mexico, Utah, and Colorado meet.

Their northerly route took them to the vicinity of modern Rangely in northwestern Colorado. The group then headed west as far as Utah Lake. There Escalante noted his Native American hosts' description of the Great Salt Lake:

> The other lake with which this one communicates, according to what they told us, covers many leagues, and its waters are noxious and extremely salty, for the Timpanois assure us that a person who moistens any part of his body with the water of the lake immediately feels much itching in the part that is wet.

The expedition turned southwest. The men nearly died of thirst in what is now known as Escalante Valley. Near present-day Cedar City, Utah, they calculated—relatively accurately, being only 2 degrees off—that continuing directly west would bring them to Monterey. On

Routes of Expeditions in the Southwest and California, 1769–1793

Gaspar de Portolá and Father Junípero Serra, 1769

Juan Bautista de Anza, 1774–1775

Father Francisco Garcés, 1775–1776

Fathers Francisco Atanasio Domínguez and Silvestre Vélez de Escalante, 1776–1793

Zuni Native group

© Infobase Publishing

The goal of the California mission system was not only religious conversion to Catholicism but also to integrate local Native Americans into the Spanish empire. Franciscan friars traveled throughout the southwest and along the California coastline claiming the land for Spain and building missions.

October 4, a blizzard convinced Escalante and Dominguez to turn back to Santa Fe. The expedition headed south toward Arizona. They eventually reached the Colorado River near Marble Canyon.

On November 26, 1776, the expedition reached Zuni pueblo, south of modern-day Gallup, New Mexico. "Not having sufficient strength to continue," the group rested. Then they continued on to Santa Fe to present their report on the lands and people they had seen. They were the first Europeans to explore the Great Basin Desert. They blazed part of what would later be called the Old Spanish Trail between Santa Fe and California.

In the end, the labors of Cabrillo, Drake, Vizcaíno, Kino, Anza, Garcés, the Dominguez-Escalante expedition, and others to open a busy route to California stalled. Bloodshed between Native Americans and colonists increased. The frontier became a dangerous place to cross. A 1781 Yuma uprising took the life of Fray Garcés. It closed the route he and Anza had opened. By then, however, Spain was more concerned with new threats arriving by sea in the Pacific Northwest.

9

Charting the Pacific Northwest The 1700s

NONE OF THE EUROPEAN POWERS SHOWED MUCH INTEREST IN exploring the Pacific Northwest until the late 1770s. It was then that they heard rumors of Russian fur traders edging down the coast. Russians had reached Alaska 50 years earlier but mainly as roving traders rather than as explorers. New European explorers set forth. They became part of an international rush to lay claim to the land between San Francisco and the Arctic.

FIRST ATTEMPTS

The first Spanish ship to investigate the rumors was the *Santiago*, commanded by Juan Pérez. Instructed by the Spanish viceroy in Mexico to find suitable sites for settlement, Pérez left the port of San Blas, Mexico, in January 1774. He reached 55° north latitude, the southeastern tip of the present state of Alaska. Then he turned south. On his return voyage, Pérez anchored near Nootka Sound, along the west coast of what was later named Vancouver Island. Like other explorers, he assumed the island was part of the mainland. Pérez traded with the Nootka people and claimed some of the land he visited. He brought back information about the native peoples, and also made contact with the Haida. They lived along the coastline north from the Queen Charlotte Islands to Prince of Wales Island.

Pérez went to sea again in March 1775 aboard the *Santiago*. This time the ship was commanded by Bruno Heceta. A second ship, the *Sonora*, was commanded by Juan Francisco de la Bodega y Quadra, who would play a major role in the region's history. The Spanish goal was to reach 65° north and to investigate rumors of a Russian presence. In early June, they stopped in northern California at a spot they named Puerto de la Trinidad, now known as Trinidad Bay. Claiming the land for Spain, the sailors spent a week with local Native Americans. The next landing, farther up the coast, was not as friendly. On July 13, near present-day Grenville, Washington, seven of Bodega y Quadra's men went ashore to get fresh water. They were killed by Native Americans, who ambushed the landing party. With the ships struggling through bad weather and the men suffering with scurvy, Heceta favored turning back. The matter was settled when the *Santiago* and the *Sonora* were separated by a storm.

Heceta retreated south toward Monterey. On August 17, his crew sighted what looked like a large bay. Heceta tried to enter it, but was driven back by a powerful current. The "bay" was actually the mouth of the Columbia River. Heceta continued on to Monterey, hoping to

In 1774, Juan Pérez became the first European to visit Nootka Sound (*above*). In 1789, Britain and Spain nearly came to war over the right to settle and trade along the Pacific coast. In 1790, an agreement known as the Nootka Convention gave both countries the right to use the area for trade.

find relief for his scurvy-ridden crew. This relief was too late for Juan Pérez, who died along the way. Meanwhile, Bodega y Quadra continued north as far as 58° north until illness and violent weather forced him to turn back.

In February 1779, Bodega y Quadra returned northward. This time, he was second in command to Ignacio Arteaga. The expedition reached nearly 60° north at Kayak Island. Near Prince William Sound a party went ashore to hold a possession ceremony. They celebrated the northernmost land ever claimed by Spain in North America. They traveled as far as Kodiak Island before they were forced back by storms and scurvy. They had failed to fulfill their orders to reach 70° north. They were also looking for Captain James Cook, unaware that the British explorer had come and gone the previous year.

CAPTAIN COOK

Captain James Cook had completed two voyages exploring the South Pacific (1768–1771 and 1771–1776). Like many others, he dreamed of finding the Northwest Passage. This water route would connect the Pacific with the Atlantic Ocean. In 1776, Cook left the South Pacific island of Tahiti and sailed north. He became the first European to visit the Hawaiian Islands (which he named the Sandwich Islands) in January 1778. He then sailed east, avoiding Spanish California and aiming at the land Sir Francis Drake called New Albion. Cook reached the coast of Oregon on March 6.

Cook called his point of landfall Cape Foul Weather. The name is still used today. The ships *Discovery* and *Resolution* struggled north through terrible storms that kept them far from the rocky coastline. Cook missed the Columbia River and the Strait of Juan de Fuca, but on March 30 he entered Nootka Sound. Cook spent a month at Nootka repairing his damaged ships and visited with the native peoples. He also explored the area, which he called King George's Sound.

Cook threaded his way through the Aleutian Islands. He sailed up the western limits of the Alaskan mainland and passed through the Bering Strait at a point Cook named Cape Prince of Wales. This land is now called the Seward Peninsula. It is the closest point on the North American mainland to Asia.

The waters were filled with ice. Cook's progress slowed to a crawl. Finally, at 70° north, Cook faced a wall of ice. On August 29, 1778, he explained his next move in his journal:

> *I did not think it consistent with prudence to make any further attempts to find a passage this year in any direction, so little was the prospect of succeeding. My direction was now directed towards finding some place where we could obtain wood and water, and in considering how I should spend the winter, so as to make some improvement to geography and navigation and at the same time be in a condition to return to the North in further search of a passage the ensuing summer.*

Cook never returned to Alaska. The *Discovery* and the *Resolution* sailed back to Hawaii. Cook was killed there on February 14, 1779, in a fight with the inhabitants. Later, his detailed journals were published in London and became bestsellers. Perhaps the greatest effect of Cook's last voyage, however, was the experience it provided George Vancouver, a lieutenant on the *Discovery*. His contributions to understanding the geography and people of the Pacific Northwest would soon surpass those of his late commander.

CONFRONTATION AT NOOTKA

European exploration in the Pacific Northwest centered on the land known today as Vancouver Island. Early explorers thought it was connected to the mainland. In late 1787, Spanish sailor Estéban José Martínez returned to Mexico from the Pacific Northwest with news. He had learned that Russian traders were planning a permanent settlement on Nootka Island, off the coast of Vancouver Island.

Martínez was ordered back to Nootka to maintain Spanish control. He returned in summer 1789. He soon encountered two ships flying the Portuguese flag. They were staffed by English traders. Martínez claimed the men were violating Spanish sovereignty and seized, then released, one of the ships. Two more English trading ships appeared, and Martínez seized them both. He then sailed for Mexico with the captured ships and crews.

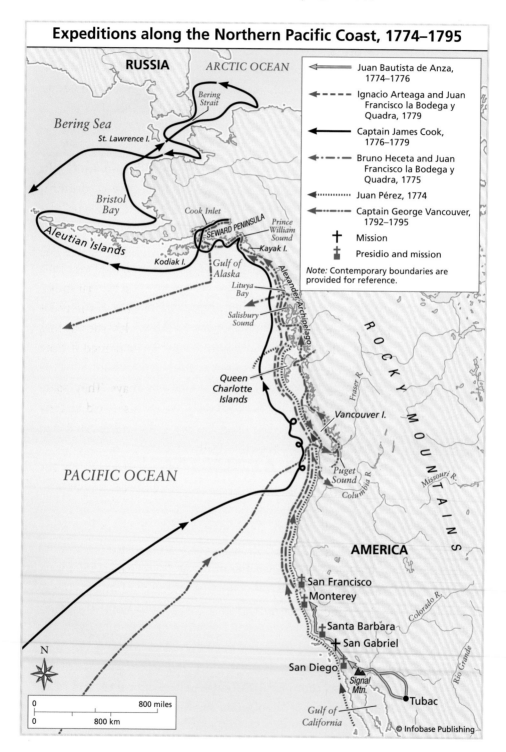

Expeditions along the Northern Pacific Coast, 1774–1795

RUSSIA

ARCTIC OCEAN

Bering
Strait

Bering Sea

St. Lawrence I.

Bristol
Bay

Aleutian Islands

Kodiak I.

Cook Inlet

SEWARD PENINSULA

Prince
William
Sound

Kayak I.

Gulf of
Alaska

Alexander Archipelago

Lituya
Bay

Salisbury
Sound

Queen
Charlotte
Islands

Vancouver I.

Fraser R.

R O C K Y   M O U N T A I N S

Missouri R.

PACIFIC OCEAN

Puget
Sound

Columbia R.

AMERICA

San Francisco
Monterey

Santa Barbara
San Gabriel

San Diego

Signal
Mtn.

Tubac

Colorado R.

Río Grande

Gulf of
California

← Juan Bautista de Anza,
1774–1776

←---- Ignacio Arteaga and Juan
Francisco la Bodega y
Quadra, 1779

← Captain James Cook,
1776–1779

←-·-·- Bruno Heceta and Juan
Francisco la Bodega y
Quadra, 1775

←········· Juan Pérez, 1774

←-··-··- Captain George Vancouver,
1792–1795

✝ Mission

✠ Presidio and mission

Note: Contemporary boundaries are
provided for reference.

N

0   800 miles
0   800 km

© Infobase Publishing

News of the incident reached England in January 1790, causing a war scare. The British government demanded compensation. Spain chose to settle the Martínez incident quickly. Their agreement, in terms favorable to Britain, is called the Nootka Convention. In it, both countries agreed to use the area as an international trading zone.

VANCOUVER ARRIVES

In April 1791, George Vancouver, who had sailed with Captain Cook, was sent to Nootka Island. Captain Vancouver was told to settle Britain's claims under the Nootka Convention and to survey the coast from California to Alaska. Vancouver reached the California coast north of San Francisco on April 17, 1792. He sailed north, mapping and charting the coastline along the way. Within weeks, the expedition turned east into the Strait of Juan de Fuca. The men began exploring its southern shore. On May 2, 1792, Vancouver's ships *Discovery* and *Chatham* entered a natural harbor near the east end of the strait. Unaware that the bay had been named Porta de la Bodega y Quadra, Vancouver named it Port Discovery after his own ship.

Vancouver's ships anchored in the bay for several days. They made repairs and collected wood and water. European diseases had already killed most of the Native Peoples. Vancouver noted in his journal that "skulls, limbs, ribs, and back bones, and other vestiges of the human body, were found in many places promiscuously scattered" on the beaches and woods surrounding deserted Native American towns.

COLUMBIA RIVER AND PUGET SOUND

While Vancouver was exploring the area, the American fur trader Robert Gray was farther south on the Pacific coast. He was near the future boundary between Oregon and Washington. He sailed into the mouth of the great river Heceta had mistaken for a bay 17 years earlier. Gray

(opposite page) In the late 1770s, the European powers began to show interest in exploring the Pacific Northwest. There were rumors of Russian presence in the region, and new explorers realized the potential for profitable land to the north.

named the river the Columbia, after his ship. This discovery was the foundation for later U.S. claims to the Oregon Territory.

On his voyage north from California, Vancouver missed the Columbia River. When he learned of Gray's discovery, Vancouver sent William Broughton to investigate. Broughton explored and surveyed 100 miles (160.9 km) of the Columbia. He found that it was not the transcontinental waterway Vancouver sought.

Meanwhile, Vancouver continued to explore the region's coast. He explored a large bay, naming it Puget Sound after his lieutenant, Peter Puget. Puget had explored the reaches of the waterway south of present-day Tacoma, Washington. Vancouver's large ships, the *Discovery* and the *Chatham*, were too large to enter shallow waters for surveying, so smaller boats were frequently used to collect the desired data.

On June 22, Vancouver encountered two Spanish ships. They were captained by Cayetano Valdés and Dionisio Alcalá Galiano. The Spanish officers were under the command of Alejandro Malaspina, an Italian-born aristocrat and captain in the Spanish navy. Like Vancouver, Malaspina had been ordered to look for a northwest passage. After exploring the coast of Alaska from Prince William Sound eastward and visiting Nootka Sound, he had returned to Mexico. In 1792, Malaspina ordered Alcalá Galiano and Valdés to sail to the Pacific Northwest and explore the Strait of Juan de Fuca. The Spanish presence was a shock to Vancouver.

Instead of competing, however, the two expeditions exchanged information and compared maps. Vancouver invited the two Spanish officers to join him in exploring northward. They accepted, but the Spanish ships could not keep up with the larger English vessels.

The English and Spanish ships soon parted. Vancouver sailed along the northeastern coast of Vancouver Island. He stopped at the Arran Rapids, powerful whirlpools caused by tidal currents. A small party, led by Lieutenant James Johnstone, was sent ahead. The group reached the Queen Charlotte Strait, which leads into the open ocean. Vancouver took his ships north through what are today called Discovery Passage, Johnstone Strait, and the Queen Charlotte Strait. He had proved that the large landmass to his left, Vancouver Island, was indeed an island.

When Vancouver arrived at Nootka, the Spanish representative there was Bodega y Quadra. They found that the agreement was not clear enough about who ruled the area. The two explorers became friends, however, so they wrote to their governments for clearer instructions. While awaiting new orders, Vancouver sailed on to the Hawaiian Islands for the winter.

THE NOOTKA CONVENTION

The first version of the Nootka Convention was signed on October 28, 1792. One of its aims was to settle damages for Spanish mariner Estéban José Martínez's confiscation of British property. The agreement also tried to define the larger question of who owned Nootka Island and the surrounding area:

> It is agreed that the buildings and tracts of land situated on the northwest Coast of the Continent of North America, or on islands adjacent to that continent, of which the subjects of His Britannic Majesty were dispossessed about the month of April 1789 by a Spanish officer [Martínez], shall be restored to the said British subjects. . . . It is agreed that the places which are to be restored to British subjects by virtue of the first article as well as in all other parts of the Northwest Coast of North America or of the islands adjacent, situated to the north of the parts of the said coast already occupied by Spain wherever either of the two powers shall have made settlements since the month of April 1789, or shall hereafter make any, the subjects of the other shall have free access and shall carry on their commerce without disturbance or molestation.

Bodega y Quadra and Vancouver could not agree on the convention's meaning when they met in September 1792. For his part, Vancouver stated in his journal that orders regarding the surrounding territories were "entirely silent as to the measures I was to adopt for retaining them afterwards." A final version of the agreement was signed January 11, 1794. In March 1795, Spain handed the island over to Britain, however, both nations abandoned their crude settlements there. It was left to future diplomats to haggle over ownership of Vancouver Island and the Pacific Northwest territories.

VANCOUVER RETURNS

Vancouver returned to the Pacific Northwest in spring 1793. He surveyed the islands at the southeastern tip of present-day Alaska. Alaska Natives attacked one of his small boats. Some of the men were nearly killed. Relations with Alaska Natives were generally "cheerful," Vancouver noted in his journal, so he was surprised by the ambush. "Whether their motives were rather to take revenge on us for injuries they may have suffered from other civilized visitors," Vancouver theorized, "or whether they conceived the valuable articles we possessed, were easily to be obtained by these means, is difficult to be determined." The expedition headed south. They made friendly stops at Spanish settlements along the California coast. Then they returned to the Hawaiian Islands.

Vancouver's third and final expedition returned to the coast of Alaska in April 1794. He went farther north than he had before. He sailed first to Cook Inlet on the south-central Alaskan shore. He worked his way southeast to Baranov Island. He named his final landfall Point Conclusion. Then he set sail for home. Vancouver arrived in England in late 1795. He had spent nearly six years exploring and ultimately circumnavigating the globe.

The years at sea took a toll on Vancouver's health. He started writing an account of his travels. He was within pages of completing it when he died on May 12, 1798. He was 40 years old. His brother John finished the work, and it was published in 1798 as *A Voyage of Discovery to the North Pacific Ocean and Round the World*. It included three volumes of journals and detailed maps. The journals contained details about the plants and animals he saw. They also contained descriptions of native tribes.

One lasting result of the voyage came from Vancouver's friendship with Bodega y Quadra. The Spaniard had suggested that Vancouver name "some port or island after us both, to commemorate our meeting." Vancouver decided, "I named that country the island of Quadra and Vancouver; with which compliment he seemed highly pleased." The name was later shortened to Vancouver Island. Their friendship was evidence that, in the final decades of the 1700s, exploration of the Pacific coastline was a genuinely international endeavor.

10

The New World in 1800

THREE HUNDRED YEARS AFTER COLUMBUS LOOKED FOR A WESTWARD route from Europe to Asia, explorers were still examining what he had actually found. Searches for gold and religious missions continued, however, they were on a much smaller scale. Expeditions were now just as likely to be driven by desire for scientific knowledge. New exploration was also driven by desire for political superiority. The world had changed since the days of the gold-hungry sailors of Columbus's second voyage, who intended to return home to Europe as rich men. Exploring the Americas was no longer a temporary adventure. New societies now existed in the Americas. Old World and New World civilizations interacted in ways whose effects are felt even today.

DESCRIBING THE KNOWN WORLD

Much of what was unknown about Earth had become clearer by the 1800s. Maps were increasingly accurate, thanks to the experience of hundreds of mariners. The Atlantic and Pacific oceans were now regions to be crossed, not underworlds filled with unknown terrors. Although ships were much improved, sailors still depended primarily on wind power. Yet, steam-and-sail combinations were starting to come into use. Beginning in 1812, steamboats moved up and down the Mississippi River. The first transatlantic steamship crossing of the Atlantic Ocean followed, in 1819.

A desire for more specific knowledge about Earth replaced hunts for gold, conquest, and global religious dominance. The size of Earth was less of a mystery than it had been in 1492, but experts still debated its shape. French scientists believed that the globe was flattened at the equator. British scientist Sir Isaac Newton calculated that it was flattened at the poles. Explorers eventually proved Newton's theory was correct.

Instead of weapons and armor, explorers carried scientific instruments. They measured the depths of rivers. They observed and collected plants and animals. Then they published accounts of their expeditions.

DISCOVERY AND THE ENLIGHTENMENT

Scientific exploration in 1800 followed a century of an intellectual movement called the Enlightenment. People attempted to understand the natural world using reason and scientific evidence. They no longer turned to religion for all the answers. As Europeans became more concerned with understanding the New World, the scientific revolution accompanying the Enlightenment in the 1600s and 1700s gave explorers an increasing array of tools for trying to make sense of the Americas and, for that matter, anywhere else they traveled. Advances were made in geology, botany, biology, and other natural sciences, especially after the mid-1600s. Improved surveying instruments produced better maps. Taxonomy and nomenclature—the classifying of plants and animals— were formalized in the 1700s.

Science in the 1700s helped explorers understand what they found. It also helped navigators get them there. For centuries sailors were unable to accurately determine longitude. English scientist John Harrison solved the problem in the 1750s with the invention of the marine chronometer. Harrison's invention—essentially an accurate pocket watch—allowed navigators to find longitude by comparing the difference between their time and what time it was at 0 degrees longitude, the prime meridian. They were then able to figure out each hour of difference represented 15 degrees of longitude. Its usefulness was proved by Captain James Cook's second voyage (1771–1776), which produced charts so accurate that navigation and cartography developed to new and improved standards. The actual geographical shape of the Americas—and much of the rest of the world—could now be seen. These maps contained details the navigators of Columbus's time would have marveled over.

SPAIN FADES FROM THE SCENE

The opening of the Americas produced a new understanding of the world. The civilizations involved underwent great changes between Columbus's time and 1800, however. Within 50 years of the Europeans' arrival, the two most powerful empires in the Americas—the Aztec and the Inca—had been smashed, and the Spanish took control. By 1800, however, Spanish power in the Americas was weakening fast. The Spanish economy was a mess. A yellow fever epidemic swept the country that year, killing thousands of people. Mountains of gold and silver from Mexico and Peru had been wasted fighting wars in Europe. Spain lost both western Florida to Britain and the Louisiana Territory to France in 1763 and 1801, respectively. Two years later, in April 1803, French leader Napoleon Bonaparte sold the 820,000-square-mile (1,319,662-sq-km) Louisiana Territory to the United States for $15 million. Five years after the Louisiana Purchase, Bonaparte overran Spain itself in his ongoing war against Britain.

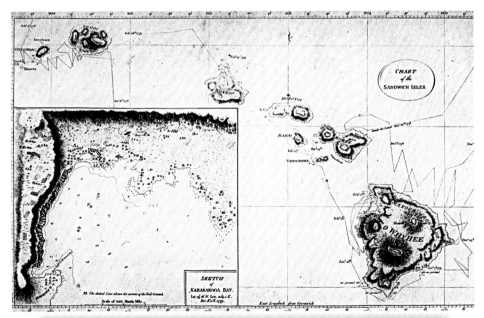

Cook mapped the west coast from California all the way to the Bering Strait, on the way claiming Cook Inlet in Alaska. He also became the first European to visit the Hawaiian Islands, which he named the Sandwich Isles. Above, Cook's chart of the Sandwich Isles shows Owhyhee (Hawaii), Mowee (Maui), Woahoo (Oahu), and a sketch of Karakakooa Bay.

In 1800, Spain also faced problems in its overseas colonies. The religious excitement that drove exploration had disappeared long ago. By 1800, many people in the New World considered themselves natives of the Americas. They wanted more power to govern themselves. Over the next 20 years, revolutions ended Spanish control of Colombia, Ecuador, and Venezuela. In 1820, Mexico seceded (separated) from Spain. The people of Brazil declared their independence from Portugal in 1822. Spain's three centuries of control in the Americas were ending in all but a few places, such as Cuba and Puerto Rico.

NEW PARTICIPANTS

New North American exploration was also poised to begin under the sponsorship of another country created by colonial discontent—the United States of America. On February 28, 1803, two months before the Louisiana Purchase, President Thomas Jefferson obtained congressional approval to send Captain Meriwether Lewis on a journey across the North American continent. Jefferson outlined the basic purpose of the expedition in a June 20, 1803, letter to Lewis:

> *The object of your mission is to explore the Missouri River, and such principal streams of it, as, by its course and communication with the waters of the Pacific Ocean, whether the Columbia, Oregan, Colorado, or any other river, may offer the most direct and practible water-communication across the continent, for the purposes of commerce.*

Lewis and William Clark led a four-year expedition. They traveled from St. Louis to where the Columbia River meets the Pacific Ocean. The expedition was the first U.S. government survey of natural resources in the American West. As they traveled, the men collected as much information as possible about Native American nations.

Not all exploration of the Americas took place in the United States. The British navy also paid for naval expeditions. In the 1800s, many of these voyages took place in the Arctic. Smaller efforts were sponsored by fur trading companies. They found routes across the Canadian Rocky Mountains.

THE CHANGED FACE OF THE AMERICAS

Between 1492 and 1800 the opening of the Americas influenced—and was influenced by—great changes. These included a more accurate understanding of global geography, ease of navigation, the improvement of scientific methods, and even the fate of nations. Many of the most profound changes took place in ways people led their lives in the steadily shrinking world.

Only a few centuries had passed after the Taino Indians and Columbus awkwardly greeted each other with sign language on the Bahamian shore at Guanahaní; since then, Native American languages were gradually replaced or diminished by European ones. By 1800, Brazilians primarily spoke Portuguese. Spanish was spoken in Mexico, Central America, and much of South America and the Caribbean. French was spoken in parts of Canada, Louisiana, and certain islands of the Lesser Antilles. English was spoken in Canada and the United States.

European languages transformed communication in the New World. However, they did not entirely destroy what had existed before. Nahuatl, the Aztec language, is still spoken in parts of Mexico and Guatemala. Quechua is spoken today in Peru, Ecuador, and Bolivia. Guarani and Spanish are the national languages of Paraguay. Words from these languages are now a part of English. Examples include raccoon, opossum, coyote, skunk, squash, tomato, potato, tobacco, Eskimo, hammock, canoe, moccasin, and totem. The slave trade brought West African words to the Caribbean and South America as well as the United States. Immigration to the Americas in the 1800s caused languages to continue changing to meet the need to communicate.

ANIMALS AND PLANTS

Transatlantic exchanges of animals and plants caused changes across the globe, affecting cultures and economies. Prior to the Spanish arrival, the only domesticated work animals in the New World were dogs and llamas. The Europeans brought pigs, sheep, cattle, and horses. These animals changed how and what Native Americans ate, wore, traveled, and traded. Escaped cattle from herds in Argentina and the southwestern United States would breed in the wild. They provided foundations for beef and leather businesses in the 1800s. In the century that followed, however, the bison—so plentiful and so crucial for the Native Peoples of North America—was all but wiped out.

Many European crops did not exist in the Americas before 1492. These included onions, melons, radishes, lettuce, cabbage, cauliflower, chickpeas, apples, peaches, pears, yams, rice, wheat, and other grains. Several crops, such as sugar, bananas, and coffee, would eventually

HORSES RETURN TO THE NEW WORLD

The ancestors of the modern horse had roamed the Americas millions of years ago. However, horses had been extinct there for many thousands of years by 1493. On his second voyage, Columbus brought many horses. "The Spaniards brought along a great many of their best horses, fleet of foot and capable of bearing armor," one of Columbus's party wrote to Nicoló Syllacio, a Sicilian philosopher. "Their formidable appearance did not fail to terrify the Indians. For they suspected that the horses fed on human flesh." Such confusion was common throughout the Americas.

In the 1600s, a profound change began. Horses accompanied the first Spanish explorers but did not reproduce in any great numbers. As colonizers pushed northward into Mexico and what is now the southwestern United States, settlers allowed horses to range freely. A similar system was used during the slower movement of Europeans into South America. The horse population increased rapidly over the next 200 years. Horses transformed Native American life from the Canadian prairies to the grasslands of Argentina. North American Great Plains tribes, which depended on the buffalo for survival, were able to hunt more easily. Societies that previously traveled on foot and transported their belongings on travois frames hitched to dogs became more mobile, moving faster and over longer distances. Horses also changed the nature of warfare. Within a few centuries, the horse changed from being an object of terror into a creature whose great contributions to Native American culture were honored in religious rituals and art across the hemisphere.

become major exports from the Americas. Meanwhile, New World crops unknown in Europe before 1492 included maize (corn), tomatoes, pumpkin, squash, sweet potatoes, pineapples, avocados, and many varieties of beans. Cacao beans were used for making chocolate. Potatoes were also new to Europe. When first imported to Europe in the 1500s, potatoes were unpopular. In time, they became such a popular food staple that future waves of colonists brought potatoes with them to North America. Peanuts and cassava (also called manioc) would become staple crops in Africa. For Europeans, the Americas became a major source of cotton. Previously, it had been available only from Asia.

In addition to such foods that now provide basic nutrition to peoples around the world, the Americas provided foods that add variety to people's diets. These included nuts such as the brazil nut, cashew, pecan, and walnut; berries such as the blackberry, blueberry, cranberry, gooseberry, raspberry, and strawberry; and many other plants, including the chili pepper, guava, Jerusalem artichoke, papaya, sugar maple, sunflower, and vanilla. Two of the most important New World crops could not be eaten. Still, they had great economic impact. By 1800, tobacco was one of the most profitable plants in the world. In the twentieth century, chicle became the basis of the vast market in chewing gum.

AFRICA IN THE NEW WORLD

Much injustice, though, would surround the introduction of some crops to the New World. The fortunes made by cultivating and shipping sugar, rice, tobacco, and cotton encouraged the growth of a slave trade that changed the course of history in Africa, as well as Europe and the Americas.

In 1492, Portuguese slavers ran the European slave trade. Since the 1440s, they enslaved West Africans and shipped them to sugar-producing areas such as the Canary Islands (off the northwest coast of Africa) and Madeira (islands located between Africa and Portugal). In the Americas, the first slaves were the native peoples of the Caribbean. Many were shipped against their will to Spain. Columbus himself was reprimanded for shipping Carib prisoners for use as slaves. Within a generation, however, the population of the Caribbean was so reduced by

In the sixteenth century, the European settlers in the New World found that fortunes could be made on sugar, rice, tobacco, and cotton crops. Yet the population of the Caribbean Indians was decreasing due to European illnesses and war. To meet the demand for labor, Africans from West and Central Africa became the source for the slave trade.

European diseases and war that a new labor source was sought. The first African slaves were shipped to Spain's American colonies in 1510.

The practice of slavery existed in the Americas before Columbus's arrival, notably in Maya, Aztec, and Inca societies. The new European slave trade, however, expanded it with horrific efficiency. It invited the participation of anyone by its commerce in human misery—African slave traders; European owners and captains of slave ships; sugar, tobacco, and cotton plantation operators throughout the islands and countries of the Western Hemisphere; and the factory and mill owners of Europe. By 1800, abolitionists in the United States and Europe openly challenged the legality of slavery. Yet, it was not declared illegal in all of the Americas until late in the nineteenth century. The Thirteenth Amendment to the Constitution banned slavery in the United States in 1865. Abolition came later to Cuba (1886) and Brazil (1888).

Africans brought to the Americas against their will had changed the New World by 1800. The Spanish presence in Mexico and Central America had created people and cultures that were distinctly mestizo, a mixture of Native American and European elements. The culture of the Caribbean had a mix of African and European elements. Patterns of African speech, religion, music, art, and other cultural elements were firmly established in the Caribbean, South America (particularly Brazil), and the United States.

CREATING A NEW WORLD

Three centuries of exploration, conquest, and colonization helped much of the world forget about Christopher Columbus after his final voyage. In the 1800s, however, people began trying to understand how they fit into the course of world history. Historians in the Americas began rediscovering Columbus. At the same time, they began discovering a new sense of themselves.

By 1800, the patterns that would determine life—and exploration—in the nineteenth-century Americas were in place. Terrible new conflicts and some surprisingly cooperative exchanges would occur with Native Americans. Explorers concentrated on opening the interior of the American hemisphere. Many motives drove new generations of explorers into unfamiliar territory. Explorers of the 1800s would not approach the Americas as exotic lands to be visited and abandoned but as lands that were their own.

Chronology

1492–1493   Christopher Columbus departs on his first voyage from the port of Palos in southern Spain on August 3, 1492. Hoping to reach Asia, Columbus lands on the islands of Cuba, Hispaniola, San Salvador, and Guadeloupe. Arrives back in Palos on March 15, 1493.

1493–1496   Columbus departs Cadiz on second voyage to reach Asia on September 25, 1493. Names island chain now known as the Lesser Antilles, then

Timeline

1513
Vasco Núñez de Balboa becomes first European to see the Pacific Ocean

1519–1522
Survivors of Ferdinand Magellan's expedition are the first to sail around the world

1492
1543

1492–1493
Christopher Columbus's voyage across the Atlantic leads to awareness of the Americas and its inhabitants. Spanish colonization begins

1530–1533
Francisco Pizarro conquers the Inca Empire and founds Lima, Peru

1542–1543
Juan Rodríguez Cabrillo and Bartolomé Ferrer claim for Spain 1,500 miles of California coastline

sights Virgin Islands and Puerto Rico. He is still convinced that Cuba is a Chinese peninsula.

1498 Columbus departs on his third voyage on May 30. He hopes to find great riches for the Spanish court. Columbus takes southerly route, crossing the Atlantic Ocean close to the equator. Discovers Trinidad and becomes first European to set foot on South American mainland when he lands on Venezuela.

1502–1504 Still convinced that Cuba is part of China, Columbus sets out on his fourth voyage on May 11, 1502. His goal is to find a strait that would lead him from the Caribbean into the Indian Ocean. Although he discovers Martinique and

1682
Robert de La Salle claims La Louisiane, territory from Illinois to the Gulf of Mexico, for France

1803–1807
William Clark and Meriwether Lewis travel overland from St. Louis to the Pacific coast in first U.S. government-sponsored survey of American West

1577

1807

1577–1580
Francis Drake becomes the first captain to circumnavigate the world and survive the journey

1687
Father Eusebio Kino establishes his first mission along the San Miguel River; he later proves that Baja California is not an island

other islands, he returns to Spain unsuccessful in finding a strait to China or having found anything of material worth.

1513
Vasco Núñez de Balboa becomes first European to see the Pacific Ocean on September 27.

◆ Ponce de León searches for the fountain of youth. Lands south of present-day Daytona Beach, Florida. León's expedition is the first from Europe to encounter the Gulf Stream.

1519
Alonso Álvarez de Pineda accidentally discovers the Mississippi River.

1519–1521
Hernán Cortés conquers the Aztec Empire and brings much of present-day Mexico under Spanish control. Thousands of Native Americans are killed by smallpox, measles, and other diseases that European explorers brought to North America. Later discovers Baja California peninsula.

1519–1522
Survivors of Ferdinand Magellan's expedition are the first to sail around the world.

1528–1536
Álvar Núñez Cabeza de Vaca and three other survivors of failed Narváez expedition are enslaved by Native Americans, then travel on foot from tribe to tribe as medicine men. De Vaca explores what is now known as the state of Texas and parts of New Mexico and Arizona. De Vaca finally reaches New Spain and returns to Europe in 1537.

1530–1533
After two failed expeditions, on his third voyage, Francisco Pizarro conquers the Inca Empire and founds Lima, Peru.

1538–1542
Hernando de Soto explores much of present-day southeastern United States.

1542
Francisco de Orellana sails the length of the Amazon River in search of gold. Orellana and his men battle a large group of female Native warriors, like the mythological Amazons. They arrive at the river's mouth on August 24.

1540–1542
Hoping to conquer the mythical "Seven Cities of Gold," Francisco Vázquez de Coronado explores

the southwestern United States. Instead of the cities of gold described by Friar Marcos de Niza, Coronado found simple pueblos constructed by the Zuni Indians. The expedition reaches the Grand Canyon and the Colorado River.

1542–1543 Juan Rodríguez Cabrillo and Bartolomé Ferrer explore 1,500 miles (2,414 km) of California coastline and claim it for Spain.

1577–1580 Given unofficial permission by Britain's Queen Elizabeth I to voyage to the Pacific coast to raid Spanish treasure ships, Francis Drake becomes the first captain to circumnavigate the world and survive the journey.

1602–1603 On a mission to find a safe harbor for the Manila treasure ships returning to Spain, Sebastián Vizcaíno renames many of the places in California previously named by Cabrillo, Ferrer, and others.

1682 Robert de La Salle claims territory from Illinois to the Gulf of Mexico for France. He names it La Louisiane, in honor of King Louis XIV.

1687 Jesuit missionary, Father Eusebio Kino establishes his first mission along the San Miguel River in northern Sonora (northwestern Mexico). Later, he leads overland expedition from Arizona to Baja California, proving that Baja California is not an island.

1774 Juan Pérez commands the *Santiago*, the first Spanish ship to investigate the rumors of Russian and English presence in the Pacific Northwest. He reaches the southeastern tip of present-day Alaska.

1790 In an agreement known as the Nootka Convention, Spain and Britain (who both try to claim Nootka Island, off the coast of present-day Vancouver Island) agree to use Nootka Sound as an international trading zone.

1791–1795 George Vancouver explores the Pacific Northwest, including the shores of Alaska, British Columbia, Washington, and Oregon. Vancouver charts the coastline's features on maps that were used by later explorers.

1803–1807   William Clark and Meriwether Lewis travel overland from St. Louis to the Pacific coast in first U.S. government-sponsored survey of American West.

Glossary

adelantado—An office conferred by the Spanish crown granting an individual the right to conquer and settle new overseas territories, in return for economic privileges and the power to administrate local government and military activities on behalf of the king of Spain.

adobe—A mixture of straw and clay that, when shaped into bricks and baked in the sun, was used by the Native Americans of the southwestern United States (including the Hopi, Zuni tribes and the Pueblo peoples) to build homes and walls, especially those often called pueblos (Spanish word for "village").

astrolabe—An early scientific instrument that enabled navigators at sea to calculate roughly their distance north of the equator by determining the altitude of the North Star over the northern horizon.

brigantine—A relatively small two-masted sailing vessel.

celestial navigation—Method used by marine navigators to calculate their location using time and the position and altitude of celestial bodies such as stars and planets and mathematical tables.

cíbolo—The Spanish word for the male American buffalo, or bison. (*Cíbola* is the female.) It appears that the name derives from the legendary "golden" city of Cíbola sought by Coronado's expedition.

entrada—The Spanish term for expedition. It literally means "entrance" or "entry."

estuary—The area where the current of a river's mouth meets ocean tides.

Franciscan—A member of the Order of Saint Francis of Assisi, a Catholic brotherhood whose members are dedicated to poverty, celibacy, and spreading Christianity through missionary work. Franciscan missionaries would often accompany Spanish explorers upon orders of the Spanish crown to carry out the expedition's religious goals.

fray—The title given by the Spanish to a Franciscan friar, it is derived from the Latin word *frater*, or "brother."

galleon—Full-rigged, heavily armed sailing vessels used primarily as treasure ships, developed in Spain in the 1500s. Galleons were essential to trade between Spain and its colonies in the Americas and the Philippines.

isthmus—A narrow neck of land connecting two larger bodies of land, such as the Isthmus of Panama.

Jesuit—A member of the Society of Jesus, a Catholic order whose missionaries dedicate themselves to preaching and higher education. Jesuit missionaries were active in the southwestern United States and Mexico until their expulsion in 1767 by order of Spain's King Charles III.

latitude—The distance north or south of the equator measured in degrees. The equator is 0 degrees.

league—A measure of distance. At the time of the early exploration of the Americas, a league was used by different nationalities to refer to a variety of distances, but it was generally defined as being slightly more than two and a half miles. Today it is commonly valued as being 3 miles (4.8 km) in length.

longitude—Standard of measurement describing the distance east or west from the meridian, a fixed north-south line depicted on maps with a baseline of zero longitude. See *meridian.*

mesa—A land formation common in the southwestern United States, with steep sides and a flat top. *Mesa* means "table" in Spanish.

mestizo—The Spanish word for "mixed," referring to a person of mixed Native American and European ancestry.

presidio—A Spanish military fort.

privateer—A privately owned ship or its captain licensed by royal authority or any government to attack enemy ships. The privateer's crew was then allowed to retain a proportion of the profits from any ships captured.

pueblo—A multistory stone or adobe Native American dwelling or the community living in such dwellings. Pueblo, which means "village" in Spanish, is also used to collectively describe tribes who live in pueblos.

quadrant—An early nautical instrument that, when sighted on the North Star, was used to find the altitude of stars and thus roughly determine latitude.

sextant—An instrument used to measure the altitude of celestial bodies and thus determine latitude. Sextants replaced astrolabes and quadrants as navigational tools.

sovereign—As a noun, it refers to the person or persons (such as a king and/or queen) who exercise total authority. As an adjective, it indicates complete authority.

speculator—A person who invests in projects and/or engages in the buying and selling of materials where there is considerable risk but who hopes to make a solid profit.

travois—A V-shaped wood pole frame drawn by dogs (and later horses), which Native Americans used to transport goods or people before horses became part of their culture.

tributary—A river or stream that flows into another larger river. It can also be used to denote a person who gives tribute or taxation in some form to a more powerful controlling body.

war dogs—Dogs trained by the Spanish military to be used as vicious attack weapons.

Bibliography

Adorno, Rolena. *Guaman Poma: Writing and Resistance in Colonial Peru.* Austin: University of Texas Press, 2002.

Ballantine, Betty, and Ian Ballantine. *The Native Americans.* Atlanta: Turner Publishing, 1993.

Cieza de León, Pedro de. *The Discovery and Conquest of Peru.* Durham, N.C.: Duke University Press, 1998.

Crosby, Alfred W. *The Columbian Exchange: Biological and Cultural Consequences of 1492.* Westport, Conn.: Praeger, 2003.

Díaz del Castillo, Bernal. *The Discovery and Conquest of Mexico 1517–1521.* New York: Da Capo Press, 1996.

Dor-Ner, Zvi. *Columbus and the Age of Discovery.* New York: William Morrow, 1991.

Dugard, Martin. *Farther Than Any Man: The Rise and Fall of Captain James Cook.* New York: Pocket Books, 2001.

Duncan, David Ewing. *Hernando de Soto: A Savage Quest in the Americas.* New York: Crown, 1995.

Edwards, Philip ed. *The Journals of Captain Cook.* New York: Penguin, 2000.

Fisher, Robin. *From Maps to Metaphors: The Pacific World of George Vancouver.* Vancouver: University of British Columbia, 1995.

Foster, William C. *Spanish Expeditions into Texas, 1689–1768.* Austin: University of Texas Press, 1995.

Garate, Donald T. *Juan Bautista De Anza: Basque Explorer in the New World, 1693–1740.* Reno: University of Nevada Press, 2003.

Hodge, Frederick W., and Theodore H. Lewis, eds. *Spanish Explorers in the Southern United States 1528–1543.* Austin: Texas State Historical Association, 1990.

Howard, David A. *Conquistador in Chains: Cabeza de Vaca and the Indians of the Americas.* Tuscaloosa: University of Alabama Press, 1997.

Kelsey, Harry. *Sir Francis Drake: The Queen's Pirate.* New Haven, Conn.: Yale University Press, 1998.

Krieger, Alex D. *We Came Naked and Barefoot: The Journey of Cabeza de Vaca Across North America.* Austin: University of Texas Press, 2002.

Prescott, William H. *History of the Conquest of Mexico and History of the Conquest of Peru.* New York: Cooper Square Press, 2000.

Preston, Douglas. *Cities of Gold: A Journey Across the American Southwest in Pursuit of Coronado.* New York: Simon & Schuster, 1992.

Ruiz, Ramón Eduardo. *Triumphs and Tragedy: A History of the Mexican People.* New York: W. W. Norton, 1992.

Sale, Kirkpatrick. *The Conquest of Paradise.* New York: Alfred A. Knopf, 1990.

Sugden, John. *Sir Francis Drake.* New York: Henry Holt, 1990.

Thomas, Hugh. *Conquest: Moctezuma, Cortes, and the Fall of Old Mexico.* New York: Simon & Schuster, 1993.

Warner, Ted J., ed. *The Domínguez-Escalante Journal: Their Expedition Through Colorado, Utah, Arizona, and New Mexico in 1776.* Salt Lake City: University of Utah Press, 1995.

Weber, David J. *The Spanish Frontier in North America.* New Haven, Conn.: Yale University Press, 1992.

Further Resources

FICTION

Card, Orson Scott. *Pastwatch: The Redemption of Christopher Columbus*. New York: Tor Books, 1997.

Clayton, Paul. *Calling Crow Nation*. New York: Berkeley Publishing Group, 1997.

Conley, Robert. *The Long Walk Home*. Norman: University of Oklahoma Press, 2000.

Conway, James. *A Mapmaker's Dream: The Meditations of Fra Mauro, Cartographer to the Court of Venice*. Boston: Shambhala, 1996.

Dorris, Michael and Louise Erdrich. *The Crown of Columbus*. Boston: G. K. Hall, 1992.

Falconer, Colin. *Feathered Serpent: A Novel of the Mexican Conquest*. New York: Crown, 2003.

Frohlich, Newton. *1492: A Novel of Christopher Columbus and His World*. New York: St. Martin's Press, 1990.

Parini, Jay. *Bay of Arrows*. New York: Holt, 1992.

VHS/DVD

Aztec Empire (2000). A&E Home Entertainment, VHS, 2000.

Biography: Christopher Columbus (2000). A&E Entertainment, VHS, 2000.

Buried Mirror: Reflections on Spain and the New World (1994). Home Vision Entertainment, VHS, 1994.

Cabeza de Vaca (1991). New Concorde Home Video, VHS/DVD, 2001.

Christopher Columbus: The Discovery of the New World (1991). PBS Home Video, VHS/DVD, 1992.

The Conquistadors (2001). PBS Home Video, VHS/DVD, 2001.

Fatal Voyage of Captain Cook (2001). A&E Entertainment, VHS, 2001.

National Geographic's Lost Kingdoms of the Maya (1993). National Geographic, Columbia Tristar, DVD, 1995.

WEB SITES

Fordham University: Colonial Latin America
www.fordham.edu/halsall/mod/modsbook08.html
A collection of historical texts for educational use.

The Mariners' Museum: The Age of Exploration
www.mariner.org/educationalad/ageofex
Materials follow maritime discovery from ancient times to Captain Cook's voyage to the South Pacific.

National Park Service, American Southwest—National Register of Historic Places Travel Itinerary
www.cr.nps.gov/nr/travel/amsw/index.htm
A series of travel itineraries that explore the United States' history through places listed in the National Register of Historical Places.

PBS Online, New Perspectives on the West
www.pbs.org/weta/thewest/program
Multimedia tour through each episode of the eight-part documentary series about the history of the American West.

University of Oregon, Juan Bautista de Anza
anza.uoregon.edu
Primary source documents and multimedia resources for students and scholars focusing on Juan Batista de Anza's two overland expeditions from the Sonoran desert to northern California.

Picture Credits

9: © Brooklyn Museum of Art/Dick S. Ramsay Fund and Healy Purchase Fund B/The Bridgeman Art Library

16: © Courtesy of the Library of Congress, [LC-USZ62-103980}

21: © North Wind Picture Archives/Alamy

25: © Infobase Publishing

28: Private Collection/Archives Charmet/The Bridgeman Art Library

34: Private Collection/The Stapleton Collection/The Bridgeman Art Library

38: © Infobase Publishing

42: © Courtesy of the Library of Congress, [LC-USZ62-104354]

45: Mansell/Time Life Pictures/Getty Images

51: © Infobase Publishing

55: American Antiquarian Society, Worcester, Massachusetts,/The Bridgeman Art Library

57: © Infobase Publishing

61: Getty Images

66: © North Wind Picture Archives/Alamy

69: Private Collection/Peter Newark American Pictures/The Bridgeman Art Library

74: © Tomasz Szymanski/Shutterstock

78: Smithsonian American Art Museum, Washington, DC/Art Resource, NY

83: © Look and Learn/The Bridgeman Art Library

87: © Mike Perry/Alamy

94: © Infobase Publishing

97: Getty Images

100: © Infobase Publishing

107: Mansell/Time Life Pictures/Getty Images

112: © Look and Learn/The Bridgeman Art Library

Index

About the Contributors

Author **TOM SMITH** holds a B.A. in English literature from Drew University and an M.A. in American history from Southern Connecticut State University. A freelance writer, researcher, journalist, and editor for more than 25 years, he has had a lifelong interest in American history. Smith has written numerous book chapters and entries about such topics as the American West, New Orleans, the environment, and historical trails.

General editor **JOHN S. BOWMAN** received a B.A. in English literature from Harvard University and matriculated at Trinity College, Cambridge University, as Harvard's Fiske Scholar and at the University of Munich. Bowman has worked as an editor and as a freelance writer for more than 40 years. He has edited numerous works of history, as well as served as general editor of Chelsea House's AMERICA AT WAR set. Bowman is the author of more than 10 books, including a volume in this series, *Exploration in the World of the Ancients, Revised Edition.*

General editor **MAURICE ISSERMAN** holds a B.A. in history from Reed College and an M.A. and Ph.D. in history from the University of Rochester. He is a professor of history at Hamilton College, specializing in twentieth-century U.S. history and the history of exploration. Isserman was a Fulbright distinguished lecturer at Moscow State University. He is the author of 12 books.